Fertile
Concrete

Fertile Concrete

By: Robert A. Douglas
Jireh Publishing Company
P.O. Box 631. Owings Mills, Maryland, 21117.
jireh.publishingco@yahoo.com

Printed and distributed in the United States of America. Published by Jireh Publishing Company. P.O. Box 631. Owings Mills, Maryland, 21117. myradicalproductions@gmail.com

Website: www.robertadouglas.org
ISBN: 978-0-9721544-9-9

Cover Designer: Morgan France-Johnson, Designer. Aesthetically Speaking. designer.aestheticallyspeaking@gmail.com

Editor: Andrew McBee

Photography: Nija Parker

To Daquan, Tayshawn, Anthony Jr., De'Asia,
Nija, Brandon, Cydnie,
Moriah,
and all the youth across the world who are our future…

The Future is Now!

Author's Note

This writing is a story that is nonfiction. Conversations are recorded and are recollected to the best of my ability.

Table of Contents

Preface   11

The Rock

First Degree   17
Tearless Crying   21
Check In, Check Out   23
Dark Waters   39
My Favorite Tie   51
A Brother Unkept   53
Broken Covenant   65
No Beauty, Just Beast   71

The In-Between

Addictions   83
Afflictions   93
Submissions   109

The Hard Place

The Countdown   123
Fertile Concrete   129

Acknowledgements   137

Preface

IF I WERE FORCED TO live this life again, I wouldn't survive. I would do things differently to avoid the trauma. I wouldn't sell drugs. I wouldn't mount the pulpit to preach either because I couldn't let the game go even after accepting my calling. But I did, and if I subtract a single situation from my life, I wouldn't be me— so I have no regrets. The events of the past, though often dangerous and detrimental to mental, physical, and emotional health, have equipped me to deal with today: the fight between the hustler I struggle to leave behind and his counterpart, the preacher living a double life in more ways than one. The ability to pen the struggles, hidden emotions, evil plots, and downfalls of the two, both past and present is their strength. It shatters the limelight of this holy being to shed some into the depths of the street kid.

People ask, "Why now?" when I've only lived for twenty-two years.

I answer this question with another, "Why not now?"

The books written by cheif executive officers promising that I too can reach their levels of success if only I apply myself can't help me—despite their strong testimonies. I search for a hope that never comes and receive false promises instead; the false promises to be the basketball player or rapper I never wanted to be.

So, "Why now?" when according to the world's standards, I am nobody who is nowhere in life. "Why now?" when I still yield to stereotypical perceptions, no matter how atypical I consider myself. I am afflicted by many issues and struggle to fight against overcoming addictions. I have yet to live up to the potential that I know lies within. The world judges me according to these weaknesses. It has good reason, but still I have something to say.

The real question is, "Am I important enough for you to listen?"

The time is now because someone, like me, is searching for one to relate to without the promises of fame and fortune. Who better than a homeless man desperate to find a way to care for the child he awaits? Someone is looking for an ear to hear or awaiting one to dare open up about the conflicting, taboo-like issues of life, even when it can be incriminating. I am that person.

Fertile Concrete is the spilled inked version of the blood pumping through the veins of a being buried deep beneath the surface of social understanding. These once concealed chambers serve as the lifeline to he who some call minister and others monster and grants access to the truths lying sealed within this tomb.

This book is about one person but more than one personality collaborating to personify this being. These few pages are the only things strong enough to contain the monster known as Lil Rob and the minister presumed to be Minister Robert A. Douglas in one place simultaneously. The two sets of chromosomes are what make up the cohesive DNA strand to he who is known to everyone as Robert Arthur Douglas.

Robert A. Douglas

The Rock

I am the man that hath seen affliction
by the rod of his wrath.
He hath led me, but I walked in darkness,
and not in light.
Surely against me is he turned;
he turneth his hand against me all the day.

–Lamentations 3:1–3

First Degree

Holding on to anger is like grasping a hot coal with the intent of throwing it at someone else; you are the one who gets burned.
–Buddha

I ASSUME YOU DON'T LIE at night excited about potentially never awakening again. Well, I do.

No, I am not suicidal—anymore—but no one lives this life or deals with these issues but me. I'm angered in hearing that someone always has it harder than me. There is truth in that, but everyone has different strengths and weaknesses, different ambitions and desires because different affects cause different effects, so how do you compare two contrasting people? In my opinion, you would have (or at least should have) killed yourself long ago having to live my life, if the gun shots didn't kill you first.

A thorough examination of what's underneath the microscope will reveal the burns of a fatherless childhood. Its eternal sizzle carries even into today. The degree is not quite deathly, but has severely severed crucial nerve endings. As a result, many other senses are enhanced, causing extreme sensitivity to other areas. The burns form a scab that peels periodically to expose the damaged area even more. Its sting is from a fire that penetrates the surface because its elements have yet to be isolated. The grinding gears from facing his abandonment cause much friction. They are accompanied by the oxygen in every inhalation taken in his absence. It also provides these combustible emotions the vital ingredient to their growth. What heats it is my misconstrued perception of what a father is to be, in regards to my future family. Tell me how to care for burns so painful that without them I'd have no motivation to ensure that my descendants do not suffer from these same scars.

Left without answers, I seek the one some call my Heavenly Father out of extreme desperation. Like my earthly one, I'd never met Him. In a book some call a love letter to His children, the Bible, I read that a good man's wealth will sustain his children's children, (Proverbs 13:22).

My earthly father must not be a good man. He is not even a real man considering that I want neither his money nor a business to succeed him in, just his wealth of time to teach me to ride my first bicycle. I'd be content with a concern to show me an example of what it takes to be a real man if not a good one. If only his wealth of experience were available to inform me that the fuzz growing around my genitals was normal, as was the discharge that stained my sheets periodically. If nothing else, I would appreciate the wealth of his friendship for me to feel comfortable discussing the time that girl took advantage of me. I didn't know whether or not to enjoy it. Either way, I didn't—neither time.

I wonder if this Heavenly Father is even a real man because apparently it's no longer a prerequisite to be any type of man before becoming a father. My father proved that. So I shouldn't get my hopes up.

This love letter that caused some uneasiness in me because

of the previous discovery also insists that I honor my earthly father and mother, (Exodus 20:10a). These words of wisdom are salt in my wounds. To honor is to respect and adhere to one's principles, by definition. Am I to honor the one who, after successfully impregnating my mother, left me in a land I consider foreign? If I indeed adhere to his principle of creating a being when unable to provide the proper care for him, I too will be considered that same sorry, trifling, black man as he. But I would argue that I'm just following the Word. No, I'm not negating biblical principle. I'm not sure what I am doing. But the confusion produces much anger, hatred, and disgust.

With oxygen, friction, and heat all present, fire is ignited by fuel, and that's my mom. Without the flammable substance she presents, these hazardous materials are only a potential threat to an explosion at most. That potential meets reality. So, in my rebellion to honor either of the two, I'm sentenced to face an untimely death: for the rest of the commandment says that long life is contingent on honoring the "honorable," (Exodus 20:10b).

I'm a mutt. Robert Arthur Robinson and Poncella Victoria Douglas are my breeders. I am also the runt of their litter of two, the first born being my older sister—Quinshawna Robinson. I assume a thoroughbred, or Robert Arthur Robinson Jr., exists somewhere, which would explain why I did not receive my father's last name. If not, I must not be deemed worthy of the title. That or Mom forbade it in hopes that I wouldn't abuse my companion as he did. Unfortunately, just a portion of him gives me his greatest propensities. When conflict arises, I flee before an alternative reaction can develop or even be considered. Ill-fatedly, he didn't stop running until running stopped him. At least I suppose it has—and the monster hopes it—but I'm uncertain if he's really alive. He's dead to me, and that's all that matters.

Before running stops me too, I compete with the thoroughbreds in this race called life as I endure yet lag behind those that are swift and strong. So I desperately search for who I am and who my father is within me in order to separate the two permanently.

Parting from that side of me won't help with the plethora of excuses I create to convince myself that running helps me escape some superfluous situation that needs be avoided. I didn't inherit that from my father, though. Instead, it stems from his counterpart, Mom, because I'm sure his conscience did not exist. He needed no excuse to escape. His own selfishness was reason enough.

I love my mother to death and loved her until her death, but I needed her to serve as a cooling agent to the burns. It was to no avail. After the abuse, the drugs, and the abandonment by my father, she returned to Baltimore, Maryland from my birthplace, Columbus, Ohio, with nothing but everything: her four-year-old daughter and her newborn baby boy, me. For what it's worth, I hear they were a family before me.

Tearless Crying

Tearless grief bleeds inwardly.
–Christian Nevell Bovee

SONGS LIKE "CHANGES," FROM 2PAC'S Greatest Hits Album, "Get Over," by Lil Wayne from Tha Carter II, and "Lose Yourself," a single for the movie 8 Mile by Eminem have sustained me through the years. Other songs similar to these produced by a hand-picked group of artists keep me today, still. So to the critics and hecklers who challenge the spirituality of a being who quotes the passages of men that fall under social and political scrutiny... welcome!

Let us neither attend to the father these men attempt to be in spite of being raised under the roofs of crack-addicted single women nor the seeds they continue to sow into their communities we Christians forsake. Instead, we should take heed of the portrayal of drugs, sex and violence without examining the roots that produce them, right? The media's depiction may contain a degree of validity, but what I know to be clear-cut is these same men saved my life time and time again. The pain that 2Pac, Lil Wayne and Eminem pour out in ways that Tupac Shakur, Shawn Carter and Marshall Mathers never could, keeps me neutralized and balanced to endure the internal battle of good and evil. Their voices feed the beast in me and are the hymns I once hid in my heart, that I might not commit the ultimate sin against God: suicide. These hymns provided the necessary stimulation to keep my mind at ease temporarily. Some are appalled by my audacity to even consider these vulgar and explicit lyrics of "violent and misled thugs" hymns. But things I hear in church sometimes give me more reason to kill myself than what I hear on the radio.

I, along with these men, share the common interest to testify to others and be that source of motivation for the one who feels he can no longer make it, because at one point I was that individual. Yet hidden agendas do exist—at least for me. I would make a hopeless effort to reach my father if pride was not a factor. If he lives, it would please me to allow the criminal to see the damage caused when he robbed me of both a childhood and aspects of life thereafter. I would inform him that it's safe to say I hate him, yet long to love him, and I despise him, but desperately need something from him. Provide me the opportunity to tell you, Mr. Robinson, I am doing well, even when I'm not, or simply rise to the occasion and offer the closure of who I am.

I soon find that closure by finding myself. Not through him, but a real man—a good man. In church, a man about eight years old comes to request prayer for his sick father to get well. As we pray, he gazes into my eyes until he breaks me, forcing me to look away. His gawk alone condemns my manhood and proves him to be more of a man than this boy more than twice his age. His father apparently embedded into his eight years of living to assume the responsibilities as the head when daddy could not. In twenty years, I still lacked what this man possessed. Though I hated what he did to me, I admire both him and his father: two real, good men.

Check-In, Check-Out

*"God grant me the serenity to accept the things I cannot change,
the courage to change the things I can, and the wisdom to know the
difference." (Serenity Prayer)*
–Reinhold Niebuhr

I AM RELIEVED TO FIND that this prayer is not
Scripture. So, I cease to pray it because the thought of being serene
at this stage of life is so distant. I can't value its worth. Since God
doesn't grant me the serenity I need, it must mean I possess the
courage to change everything—which is false for two reasons. One,
the obvious, I can't change the past and will never be at peace with
it. Two, I inevitably inherited a spirit of cowardice, so even if I wish
to confront these issues, the question is, will I?

The Bible does state that the price to pay for sins committed
is death. It too urges us to obey the Ten Commandments—one
being not to steal. But is it sin considering the intent of one's heart
and the principle of the lesser of two evils?

With Mom out catering to the piece of him that he left, a
fierce addiction to alcohol and drugs, my sister becomes a mother
to me at age five. From what I am told by my Grandma, my sister
provides me necessities by depleting mom's chemical dependency

funds. So is she held accountable for stealing in a situation where it's either sin to save a life or sin to not love her little brother as herself? Either way, I thank her for saving me from death by starvation when it was Mom's job to do so. The crack epidemic took hold of Mom. Instead of her feeding the seed she conceived and later birthed, she yielded to the seed of an addiction that my father planted in her. That is the only seed that was not taken away. At least she will always have a part of him.

One SIDS risk I was safe from, though, was crib death—I didn't have a crib to die in. Neither Mom nor Grandma had enough money for my sister to steal for that, but I don't doubt that she would've purchased that as well somehow. My sister loves me even though my birth ruined her chances at a true family. Sorry, sister.

I keep Mom's memory beneath my bosom and buried the pain with her body, but the grave re-opens every August. It is August of 1988 when she introduces me to the agony of this world at 12:36 p.m. The following August, she lets them take us. That day, I lose the one thing I truly love other than my sister. The one I felt a constant need for falls from my grasp and to me, life ends. How can I go on without the encouraging words or feeling its warm torso while I slept at night? To this day, I still miss that superhero action figure. I want to miss my mother but I don't know her.

Ten Augusts later, she punches her time clock. A few years prior, she punches me as we are walking past the Cloverland Milk Company on Exeter Hall and Loch Raven Boulevard, growing acquainted with one another. Amazed at the never ending milk towers that extend to the sky, I slightly increase my pace. Mom chases me down, jumps on me and hits me on the face.

"Don't you ever walk that far in front of me around here again, Man-Man! If something happens to you, how am I gonna protect you?"

"Protect me from what?" I asked. I was afraid to question her at first, but I had to know. I was curious.

I got up and continued on the sidewalk at her side without an answer. My face didn't sting as much as my feelings did. Some attribute the incident to the love of a mother but I say it is due to what she purchased from that ugly, dark grown-up with the dingy tank top earlier in the shopping center parking lot and the thirty minutes she spent in the bathroom at Grandma's before we left. In fact, I know because she is always pleasant to me otherwise.

Every August in between, she hates me. I can't blame her. I bring hell into her world before I even get the chance to live. Before me, she had a family that she loved and I ruined it.

It takes almost six years for me to accidently hear Mom's voice and see her face again since she gave us up. She knows my whereabouts. She handpicks the residence and guardianship for the both of us. She split us up between two of our great-aunts. My sister calls the one she lives with Aunt Eunice like the rest of her nieces and nephews. I call the one I live with Ma because she is the only mother I know. I was so young when we were removed from Mom. I forgot her. It may have been by choice and not a glitch in my mental remembrance.

The days when I am visiting Grandma are always dull. I don't like the way it smells here either. My visits consist of the same events, always: going to the store for her, sitting to watch her favorite shows on this black and white television and listening to the sweet lyrics of what her generation calls the "Oldies but Goodies." The latter of the three activities is my favorite. Michael Jackson dominates the radio and Grandma's eight track recorder. He is the man. I put his record on and take my place on the protective plastic covering Grandma's colorful couch and begin with the song "You Are Not Alone." That's my jam. His soothing voice convinces me that I will always have him with me even though I've yet to see his face (and even though that is not the intent of the song). He knows I feel alone. I feel like something is missing, but I cannot pin-point what that something is. Maybe it's my father. No, it's something more.

This house is where music lives. It takes root in my heart and becomes not just instrumental to my life, but the instruments of my life. The Luther Vandross, Teddy Pendergrass, Barry White records, to name a few, that my friends constantly ask how I know, came from Grandma's eight track recorder. When the records blare through the speakers, Grandma takes her seat next to me. She starts with closing her eyes and rubbing her thighs. Next, she picks up the pad and pen by the time the third song begins. All of this is normal. I never read what she writes. It may be her thoughts and I wouldn't want anyone to read my thoughts, so I don't do it to her. My thoughts would have me committed to a mental facility.

There is a knock at the door, not so normal. Grandma gets up and makes a sound that expresses her confusion. She isn't expecting anyone. She maneuvers her way through all of the clutter she cherishes to answer the door.

She yells, "Poncella, hey baby!"

"Hey, Ma," this Poncella replies.

They kiss.

Huh? Wait, why did she just call my Grandma, Ma? I thought I met all of Grandma's children: my uncle Antoine and Shontee, my aunt. I could be mistaken. I haven't quite figured out the concept of relation to one another in the family structure yet. For example, Ma, who I live with, refers to Grandma as her sister Delores— Grandma's middle name—instead of calling her Ma. My brother Danny calls her Aunt Delores and so does my sister Nivia. Also, Ma and Nivia's last name is Jones, Danny has his father's last name, Bowser, and I have the same last name as Grandma, Uncle Antoine and Shontee. This could make perfect sense somehow. The woman at the door is brown-skinned. That stands out to me because besides my Uncle Antoine, I am surrounded by light-skinned individuals, especially at home. None of them have this big nose that I have, except this lady that walks through the door.

Following their embrace, Poncella walks over to me gesturing for a hug and says, "Oh my God, hey Man-Man!"

She hugs me and kisses me. I get a closer look at her. Who is this woman that I am a spitting image of? More importantly, who is Man-Man? Grandma says she is my mom, but I already have one.

Back at home a few months after this incident, I find an envelope on my bunked bed, already torn halfway open. I never get mail, so I don't gripe over someone invading my privacy. It is addressed to me, from Poncella V. Douglas. The space for her address has a bunch of numbers in its place. After forsaking my sister and me, leaving me to believe that the woman who took me in was the one who birthed me, this new lady later expresses her gratitude for our custodial removal when she writes me from jail. I guess it's true that people do have time to think about the things furthest from their minds while incarcerated.

I notice a picture drawn on the back of the envelope. It is a character from a cartoon. I assume it is what she thinks is a picture of the superhero action figure I lost—cute, yet a hurtful reminder. The character she means to draw was the closest thing I had to a father. He instilled in me the virtue that I could do anything I set my mind to; sticking to it is my issue. He assured me that evil would never prevail against good. He is the father that I could honor. He spoke into my life and gave me something that my parents didn't care to: hope.

This letter explains my origins as Man-Man and is filled with patronizing apologies and promises to be the broken family my father left us to be. Though I am furious about being lied to for so long, everything in me leaps towards heaven before reading that I am no longer her only son, nor is my big sister, Quinshawna, her only daughter.

How could she? How do you justify losing your first two children for an addiction and avoiding communication with them to begin another family? I guess she needed a fresh start.

The sequence is as follows:

Mom has her first born girl.

Dad, Mom and baby girl are a family.

Mom has her first born boy.

Dad leaves Mom with the two children.

Mom elopes with the drugs she yokes herself to and releases her children from her custody.

Mom finds a new man.

Mom has her new first born girl and her new first born boy by this new man.

Their dad, my mom and their two children remain a family until her death.

This makes my birth, which I never asked for, the broken link in her life. She loved me but hated me for something I had no control over. She could have wanted to abort, but I was too strong to let go. I made it out regardless of the black lungs, the severing liver, and the deteriorating organs I depended upon. I prevailed against the entrapment of her narrow canal that probably refused to dilate and was birthed with no brain defects or chemical dependencies.

There is one minor birth defect in me though: the raging temper within. It is said by researchers that a mother who abuses drugs or alcohol while pregnant can cause the child to have chemical dependencies when born or have emotional issues and mismanaged anger problems later in life. I dodged the chemical dependency. As for the others, I was not so fortunate, and July 31st, 1999—her thirty-fifth birthday—was the last straw.

Grandma's house, full of clutter and the colorful couch, was in Waverly. It burned down, so she moved. While visiting her the weekend of Mom's birthday on Boone Street, where every house is boarded up but hers, Mom turns the corner of the alleyway as drunk as sober can be. Stumbling, cursing, and yelling, she lays eyes on me and grows instantly sedated. I shake my head and turn to leave. My ride is here to take me home to Ma.

As I get in the car, she yells, "I love you, Man-Man!"

I try to stop and respond but am forced into the back seat of a green Q45. "No, you don't, you liar," is what I want to shout at her but we are pulling off. I look back to see a tear fall from her left eye. The New York Yankees cap I accidently left on the step now rests upon her head as we drive away. She takes her seat on the step and waves goodbye to the car as if she will never see me again. I start to cry. I finally feel a mother's love and see her remorse. I know she feels the pain she causes me in her drunkenness that day and everyday prior.

Kneeling in the back seat, looking out of the rear window, I feel the same uncertainty as the day I first met her—déjà vu. She doesn't delight in my departure this time. So I grow ecstatic because her repentant face convinces me that her promise will one day come true. I write her a letter and draw a picture to show her that I remember. I dream and plan on running into her again at Grandma's house.

On Monday, August 16th, 1999, I ask Ma if I can go visit Grandma this weekend. She knows by now that I just want to see Mom. She tells me no because she doesn't have a way for me to get there. I tell her I can catch the bus. It's not like I haven't caught the bus alone before. She doesn't have any money, she says. I have money in my piggy bank. She reluctantly permits me to go seeing that I won't let up. I am on top of the world. I decide to spend my upcoming birthday with Mom too if she recognizes its rapid approach. This ten-year-old child, who only knows how to forgive, rushes through the week carelessly for the weekend. It's been a while since the last I saw her—her birthday to be exact. My lasting visual of her is her crying on the steps and waving underneath the shade of my hat.

Tuesday, August 17th, 1999, comes and goes as my newfound love for her further develops. I call Grandma everyday to be sure that Mom will show up when I arrive. She assures me Mom will.

August 20th, 1999, sparks the weekend and that very day, exactly seven days before my birthday and hours before I am to head to the bus stop, Mom dies for the second time. This death, though, is permanent and irreversible. A dream deferred. Yet again, she makes a selfish decision, this time to check out days before I am to celebrate the day she checked me in. It takes being an orphan for me to realize that I will not have the family I desire and was once promised, the family that is owed to me. My birthday present from her came early—her last words to me, "I love you Man-Man."

Mom's relatives often degrade her in my presence, both before and after her death. I wonder if it was intentional of them or did they think I wouldn't pick up on the conversation. But when I inquire about the actual cause of her death, they hide the details.

No, they lie.

I am relieved to find out that Mom died of an asthma attack and nothing else. That's what the family tells me. She had chronic bronchitis, which makes sense. I thank God that drugs did not cause her demise. My sister and I already suffered a metaphorical death from her usage of them. We need not bear the pain of her physical death from the same. But we do. And this is how I overhear the dead spoken of as I go to get the rest of my shrimp fried rice from the refrigerator:

"Well, what kind of drug was it?"

"Girl, I don't know. Ain't no telling what she was strung out on. Probably crack or something."

"Well, I was told that nigga was there with her while she was taking God knows what and when she died, he put her in the truck and took her to Delores's house."

"Mmm mmm mmm."

If my heart still beats, it is full of deoxygenized blood because I refuse to breathe the entire time. I warm up my rice but cannot eat it. All I can think of is those two little ones she loved so much, her new kids. I've seen them only a few times.

Mom nicknamed all of us. She called Quinshawna "Bug" even though Quinshawna hates that name. I asked Mom why she named her that once. When Quinshawna was around, Mom said it's because she was her lovely little lady bug. But alone, Mom told me that Quinshawna looked like a little bug when she was a baby, hence the name. She called my little sister "Angel" and my little brother

"Binky." They were seven and six when Mom died. The first time I saw them was the time Mom and I were walking past the milk company. We were headed to their house.

We arrived on Carswell Street. Their house was halfway down the block. Mom walked up the steps and opened the unlocked door. It was summer time. The windows read Merry X-Mas. There were no curtains. All I can recall about the inside is the bathroom in the basement. I remember because I used it. There was a bath tub that stood on its own bottom. I remember because as I peed into the toilet, I saw a huge rat run behind that tub and into a hole.

Binky takes to me instantly as his big brother. We resemble one another so much so that the only major distinctions are height, weight and hair texture. He has pretty curly hair. Mine grows straight out and stands at the top of my head as if I carry an overload of electricity in me. It takes time for Angel to warm up to me. But it isn't long before she is begging me for back rides every time she sees me. That's my little brother, my little sister, and I love them. I see them more than I see Quinshawna.

The night of Mom's death, I reflect on my little time with them and wrestle with God, telling Him that I will care for her kids to the best of my ability if He just releases His hatred for me. I suspect I am victorious until August, 26th, 1999 when I am informed that my younger siblings moved to Virginia, missing the funeral and leaving me never to see them again. If God does exist, He must take vacation in August because its torture doesn't stop there.

"There's no more space in the limo for you, young man. You have to find someone else to ride with."

Who is this man, and who grants him the authority to dictate my means of transportation to my mother's funeral? Who, besides my sister and Grandma, is more important than me to have privilege to this luxurious ride? It isn't that it's my mother's funeral that upsets me but I've never ridden in a limo before. I just stand silent, squinting my eyes at the mortician and frowning—not to intimidate him, even though it seems to have that effect, but because the sun melts the grease on the parts in my head and it slides down into my eyes. It burns. He looks away and lets out a sigh.

"My little Brova is riding in this limo, sir! C'mon Brova," demands Sista, Quinshawna.

She never calls me by my name. That's something she and Mom had in common. I assume neither one of them wanted to hear my father's name anymore. Her choice term of endearment is Brova. So I call her Sista. She doesn't let me call her Bug.

Sista yanks me and doesn't release my pencil thin wrist until I am crammed between the window of the limo and Grandma.

The ride to the church seems to take so long, which usually takes about ten minutes. Out of the window is a cloud, a cloud like no other. It looks like a puffy white ballroom for angels. The sun's beams peer through it onto the earth. It follows us the entire ride, waiting at every stop light and turning every corner with this car. I enrapt myself with this enormous cotton ball and wonder if it is the cloud that carries Mom to Heaven. Meanwhile, Grandma is soaking my shirt with her tears. Shontee is doing the same with Grandma's shirt and Sista with Shontee's. I am too distracted to participate in the ripple effect. I doubt I can produce tears at this point anyway. These people hold onto many memories with Mom.

Grandma birthed her and raised her. Shontee, Mom's sister, grew up with her and lived with her. Sista not only spent the first five years of her life with Mom but saw her much more frequently than I did. Me, I can count on two hands the number of times I saw Mom. If we speak of pleasant times, I only need one. But I cherish every second spent together.

The limo pulls to the curb and the cloud breaks loose from my optical grip and vanishes. We all enter into the New Lebanon Calvary Baptist Church, where all of my family attends.

"Your great-grandmother [Mary Blackwell] helped build this church. She held bake sales and all types of fundraisers to raise money for us to get this building that you are sitting in," is what the elderly mothers of the church tell me every time I come here. In their old age, they also reveal a potential family secret from time-to-time by saying, "The late Pastor Joseph Stewart is your great-grandfather." From what I know, Ben Blackwell is my great grandfather.

Anyway, I get a splinter every time I come here because of the chafing wooden seats. Great-Grandma Mary may have helped build it, but someone needs to come along to maintain it. Trying to be positive, I think about how good it will be for me to finally have a picture of Mom on her obituary. I rush to the usher for my final birthday present. The picture is lovely. It is as beautiful as a white dove. Actually, it is a white dove—literally. Nice: just not my mom. Whoever designed her obituary didn't select a picture for it.

I wonder why.

Fighting to bypass the anger, I march down to the altar to view Mom's corpse. The aisle stretches itself out, making this walk awkward, but the fact that my white cotton socks are on display with every step as my suit pants rise grabs my attention and passes the time.

The casket is nice. It's white with gold trimming. Judging by the way she is regarded by some, I thought she would be buried in the scrap plywood of a demolition project. Then again, Grandma wouldn't allow that.

Her outfit isn't as nice. Standing before her peering through those stitched eyelids, I feel Mom's eyes. They are warm, they get to rest. Sista stands next to me. We gaze in silence for about ten minutes. I'm afraid to touch my dead mother before me. She is so bloated. Her hair is intact, nails properly groomed. The only thing missing is her beautiful smile along with the rest of her normal self. Mom would never wear red lipstick, blush, pearls or this pink dress. I miss her smile already. There is nothing I can do now to make her smile, because she has no life in her. Her pretty teeth are sown behind her painted lips.

My mother is dead, I think to myself.

"My mother is dead," I have to say aloud.

It's so hard to believe because I feel guilty. I spent our short time together embarrassed and ashamed of her. If any of my friends tried cracking your momma jokes, I would bash their heads in when they tried to make my mother the butt of them. They didn't know why. And now, my mother is dead. I walked around talking about how much I couldn't stand her and now I am standing here missing her once she is dead. She's dead! The feminine version of myself is lying here in this casket. A part of me lies there dead with her. It is a part that can never be revived until we meet again—if we meet again. I miss my mommy.

I want her back.

Mom could find humor in any situation, so I try to think of something she would say at the time. Nothing.

The line builds behind us so I slide to the side and Sista goes to get her splinters at her seat. People pass and compliment Mom's make-up, her nice pink dress and her hair. But none of these things are her. No one seems to really know her. Following these praises, people ask for Mom's two youngest children and console Sista. Only few offer their condolences to me. No one recognizes me as Poncella's son.

"Who is that?" strangers whisper, speaking of me.

"That's her boy," pointing to Ma, others reply.

They truly believe that because I lived with my aunt and refer to her as Ma this occasion has no effect on me. I kiss Mom's icecold forehead and take my place in the pew hoping the splinters don't slice these cheap pants. The morticians close the top half of her permanent bed for me to never see my mother again. I want to jump in through that crevice before it shuts completely to have more time with her. I would try if Sista wasn't holding me so tightly. It isn't even six years since I first stood before Mom receiving her salutation and now I'm forced to say goodbye. Flesh of my flesh, blood of my blood.

I feel a tug on my right leg. It is my little cousin, Daquan, Shontee's first son. Maybe he is trying to help cover these bright socks of mine.

No, he is pulling himself up from the floor to say, "Robert, Aunt Pon-Pon gone to Heaven." I can only hope so.

That produces my first tear of the day and I soak his shirt. By the time my sobs end, the preacher is finished the sermon and giving his benediction. The church is three quarters empty. Familiar faces surround the casket, prepared to carry Mom to her lot in the graveyard.

We return to Grandma's house where everyone sits around laughing and eating Popeye's chicken. It's some type of festival that I am unaware of. My mother's death warrants some sort of celebration.

Everyone spends this occasion catching up, sharing the highlights of past years. We only see the family on Thanksgiving Day, Christmas Day and the days of funerals. Everyone tries talking to me, but I lie on the couch mute, craving eggs. It was the first and last supper Mom and I shared together.

We were at her house, the one without the curtains. I said to her, "Mom, I'm hungry."

Fumbling through the empty cabinets and refrigerator, she says, "All we have is eggs, Man-Man. I'll scramble you some. You like cheese?"

I did like cheese. But I did not like the ketchup she poured on top of my food. Remembering this, I grow ill and avoid eggs and my true emotion on the matter for years after that day.

Becoming of age, I obtain Mom's death certificate to learn of her true cause of death. Acute Verapamil Intoxication is what the autopsy renders. Verapamil is a drug that treats people with heart related issues such as heartache due to lack of oxygen or blood in the heart and for abnormal electrical activity in the heart. Physically, she had no heart condition. She resorted to prescription drugs. I speculate she felt that the only relief from the pain was to escape this world. Am I suggesting suicide? Studies show that many overdose on this medication to commit suicide. Any dosage was an overdose for her.

Extreme depression from the possibility drives me to attempt to crack the case. Her criminal background shows many battery and assault charges, her being both the victim and defendant. She also has a possession of a deadly weapon charge. All of these involve her and her domestic partner, my siblings' father. Whether suicide or premeditated murder, to this day I am uncertain of the method used to produce this result and the pain is incomprehensible.

Dark Waters

He made darkness his secret place; his pavilion round about him were dark waters and thick clouds of the skies.
-2 Samuel 22:12

WE START WITH SIX: JOHN Douglas, my grandfather; Mary Delores Douglas, Grandma; Antoine Ivan Douglas, my uncle; Poncella Victoria Douglas, Mom; Shontee Vonzella Douglas, my aunt; and Robert Arthur Douglas, me. By the time I am born, we are down to five.

The army veteran John Douglas weds Grandma (her maiden name being Mary D. Blackwell), shares the experience of birthing three children together, and dies of alcoholism before I am born, unfortunately. Today, one remains. I am he who has yet to depart this earthly tabernacle. The rest of the clan is murdered in some form or fashion. It seems as if God systematically sanctions these murders in a detailed and explicit order or at the least allows it.

I count it not happenstance that ancient humanity defined and placed meaning in the names given to their descendants. Unfortunately, the name Douglas is inescapable. Douglas is translated by the English of the seventeenth century, and from Gaelic to mean "dark waters"—which explains a lot. This pool of dark waters that my tribe bastes in is what eventually strangles the life out of the individuals trapped within.

I am convinced that my destiny will also end in the manners of this tragic generational curse of the Douglas lineage. In my twenty years, death has surely been no stranger but when it approaches, God spares me for some reason. Thankfully, my siblings and cousins, the children of Shontee, escape this kiss of death. My parents must consider Sista honorable enough to carry my father's last name. My younger siblings, Poncella "Angel" Crayton, and Crandell "Binky" Crayton, receive the last name of their father also—as do my little cousins.

Coincidence?

I think not.

Thus, I deem it right to say that I am the last samurai.

The first execution I live to experience is Uncle Antoine's— Antoine Ivan Douglas translated from Latin, Hebrew, and Gaelic to mean a praiseworthy gift from God in dark waters.

He is just that. This sky-scraping, thin, J.J.-from-Good-Timeswanna-be with that exceptionally thick mustache keeps me on his hip and offers his wealth of things I needed from my father. He is the only father-figure, or male for that matter, to own a place in my heart. Through example, he teaches me to be kind and gentle to others. He loves his only nephew. Uncle Antoine has no children of his own, so I am the closest to a son for him. So he takes me everywhere with him and shows me everything. He praises me when I excel and corrects me when I am wrong, but talks Grandma down from the beatings she stands ready to give me. I want to be just like him. When I get older, I will attend the same prestigious high school as he, Baltimore City College High School. He credits the institute every time I ask him how he grew to be so smart.

But the effects the dark waters have on him cause others to view him negatively. The drugs have very little hold on my uncle in comparison to the alcohol. He depends on it just to be able to function. Sadly, there is a thin line between functional and extreme intoxication and he frequently flirts with that border. But his heart is purer than gold and I hold a place in it that surmounts both the drugs and alcohol.

Once when visiting Grandma, she sends us both to the store for a BC and a Pepsi, our daily routine. Somehow ending up in a liquor store, a crucial addition to this routine, Uncle Antoine buys his drinks for the evening. I too want a drink, so I beg him for a V8. He's run out of money. His bag is filled with everything from the top shelf. The change from the money Grandma gave him is all he has left. He compromises it for my drink and when we return home, Grandma is convinced that Uncle Antoine bought drugs with her money. I offer my sworn testimony on his behalf but she spanks me for lying for a junkie.

That same night, I arise in my cartoon print briefs, tired. Uncle Antoine is not an angry drunk like every other drunk I know. He gets very depressed instead. I would rather him be angry. He sits at the table with his head in his hands.

I confess to him, "Um, Uncle Antoine. I want you to stop drinking and stop smoking."

Of course, I anticipate his response will be typical of a man of his particular stature. He will not only deny his problem, but yell, and discipline me for not staying in a child's place, or blatantly disregard the concerns I show for him altogether. But shockingly, he weeps. His weeping lasts about an hour as he gapes at me in shame.

He assumes I am too young and innocent to know how prevalent drugs are in his life. But drugs and alcohol are a major part of my own life indirectly. That night, he promises to leave them both alone. I believe him and believe in him—even though no one else does.

To their surprise, he returns after a year and a half hiatus, rehabilitated. He attended a facility called The Salvation Army and is employed and accompanied by his fiancée, Maria. He'd also rededicated his life to his personal Savior Jesus Christ while away and made certain to repay Grandma all he stole from her in the past. Maybe she believes him now about the night we went to the store.

Everyone sees the change in him. It is admirable. It makes me feel valued to know that my words are enough to strike change in such an individual. The adventures that lay ahead of us thrill me. His love is the closest I will ever get to feeling the love of a father. It is enough. But close soon grows far away because two short weeks after his return, Uncle Antoine is struck by a car and killed by the drunk driver. The irony sickens me. He credits his Savior for his deliverance from what could've killed him internally yet it causes another person to do the job for him. The driver of the vehicle survives. This praiseworthy gift from God does everything in his power to escape the dark waters but is knocked right back in to sink to his death by what he himself already conquered in his own life. The one man that I draw close to is now gone, leaving only the final four to remain.

The curse strikes Mom, Poncella Victoria Douglas—with her first name having no meaning but middle, translated from Latin, and last to mean a conqueror in dark waters—next.

Mom conquered many obstacles in her life. Her heart is gentle but rough enough to curse you out at the drop of a dime without a second thought thereafter. She possesses the ability to smile through anything, so she hides her pain well. Even bearing bruises and other wounds from time-to-time, she holds fast to her optimistic outlook on life. Her eyes can convince you of anything that parts her lips, so that none of her troubles are alarming to others. She isn't the transient type that has her mind set on some unattainable goal each week. All she speaks of is her dream to be a chef, nothing more. She pursued it vigorously before the age of crack-cocaine. Sadly, she couldn't conquer the dark waters in order to achieve it. The many emotions and complications wrapped up in her death limit the detail of this calamity. Although it is inconclusive whether she took the pill voluntarily or not, the prescription did indeed cause an asthma attack. However, she is not alone when she has the reaction.

From what I discover through eavesdropping, it isn't until she suffocates completely that her partner offers assistance in her final moments of distress. The man accompanying her sits and watches her die because of his own selfish desire not to have his high spoiled. Calling an ambulance could create legal issues for him, so he opts out. When she ceases to struggle, he throws Mom in the bed of his truck and drops her off at Grandma's, not the hospital.

That same day I receive the greatest tribute to my mom that anyone could dig up to offer.

"Your mother was just starting to change. For the first time, since Poncella was a child, I sent her to the store and she brought me back my exact change."

I am unsure how to feel about that. I yell and scream obscenities at God to tempt Him to respond and His reply is deafening—utter silence. He not only forsakes me but leaves me with only the triple threat for support.

Afraid for whom the curse will strike next, I spend more time with Grandma and Shontee. One major discouragement to staying with them the entire weekend is that Grandma, Mary Delores

Douglas—bitter sorrows in dark waters from Hebrew, Latin, and Gaelic translations—forces me to go to church every Sunday.

I dare not express my desire not to attend. The stern expression she wears on that constantly scrunched up light-skinned face induces enough fear in me not to voice my opinion if I don't want to find out the consequence. Grandma is old school. She whips me for the slightest reasons and wants to teach me the principles behind that whipping afterwards. Only one of them I understood enough to hold on to.

Seven years old at the time, I sit in my pajama sleeper eating a peanut butter and jelly sandwich and watching "The Price is Right" with Grandma, her favorite show. All of a sudden, I make an "uh oh."

"Robert," she snaps.

My head automatically responds before my brain can command it to, to give her the eye contact she requires. "Yes, ma'am."

"Did you use the bathroom on yourself?"

"No," I say in respectful disgust. I lied. I sit on my ankles to keep it from smashing to my bottom. I have to make an escape to the bathroom before she notices.

"Sit your butt right down," she demands. As the smell grows more potent and the last contestant on the show spins the wheel, she blurts out, "Yes you did! Get in that bathroom and get in the tub!"

I get up in shame because she knew the entire time. I do as I am told and wait patiently for her to run my water and wash me clean. It was an accident, Grandma, I thought to say in my most pitiful voice. I better not. I try crying but am amused that both the partnering villian fighting superheroes printed on my underwear have brown faces from the stains I left. She catches me snickering when she walks in. I choke on the last chuckle coming up as I swallow it back down. Grandma washes me in complete silence. She is either upset because I interrupted the end of her show or because I disrespected her nose with the smell. Finally, she breaks that silence after the water in the tub runs out.

"This is gonna hurt me more than it hurts you." She says this all of the time. Wailing on my wet, naked behind, "That's for telling Grandma a lie," she speaks over the sound of the lashes. She leaves me in the tub rolling around taking another bath in my tears. Grandma surely holds no punches, especially the ones heading towards my chest.

I suffer my greatest embarrassments with her at church which is another reason I do not wish to attend, next to my lack of interest. Once, just before evening service as we all enjoy our chicken boxes, she tells a girl there who suffers from acne if she "will just wipe her face with a soiled diaper," she could "clear that mess up," gracefully paraphrased of course. Needless to say, I continue to dread those services. Until one day, I am hired by the pastor to clean the pews when the crowd commences. The money becomes my sole motivation to attend. I surely have no desire to seek anything from a God that is so distant to me. In this state of servitude though, I reap many advantages and ponder the thought that maybe God hasn't forgot about me after all. That thought vanishes when Grandma falls down the stairs and hurts her side. The emergency room physicians discharge her with only a prescription to kill the pain.

The pain then kills her.

That night, her appendix bursts inside of her. By the time she makes it back to the hospital, it is too late. She is alive, but not for long. There is nothing the physicians can do. I don't get the chance to see her before her passing because shortly after receiving the news, the curse silences her in her pain. The fall punctured her appendix and the doctors didn't take the necessary precautions or procedures because of her lack of insurance. Somehow the cost of medical attention is of greater value than what cost me my Grandma.

Of every human that embodies this earth, I loved her the most. She was so hard on me, on everyone. She would push me in every way imaginable and though I didn't appreciate it, I miss it sincerely today. What I admire most about Grandma is the level of strength she possessed. In the loss of her first two children, she was still determined to serve her God who, she said, kept her. I thank her God, for Grandma's sake, that the curse struck her before it did Shontee or me. She wouldn't be able to bear it. I didn't want her to face more time in that mental facility like when Uncle Antoine and Mom died. As she yelped at the police, the paramedics strapped her reluctant body to a bed with wheels and took her away. I missed her while she was gone. Still, that experience didn't break her spirits or soften her personality. She made certain that while she resided on this side, she'd push me to greatness. She was very ineffective in verbal expression so she tried not to talk much. She spoke through her pen instead and published her poetic works. Those that were not lost, I hold onto dearly.

With her gone, I left New Lebanon because money couldn't keep me pretending to be a true Christian. I sat in the front row every week to receive something from God and got nothing. Besides, without Grandma hollering, "Hallelujah!" from the fifth pew every Sunday, things seemed different.

In no time, Grandma's old home turns into a stash house and I find myself transporting drugs, drinking, and smoking when I come to visit. There is always something left in the fifths of liquor left on the kitchen table. When everyone goes to sleep, I take a sip or three. Yuck! I can't understand how people drink this toxin and enjoy it. It burns my throat and chest. I didn't know at the time that these drinks should be mixed with non-alcoholic ones to both dilute it and improve the taste. Guzzling this bottle the way I am could give me alcohol poisoning, but settles for knocking me out cold. The scraps of weed, consisting mostly of seeds and stems from bagging up, fill my blunts and gets me high enough after first catching contact from the smoke filling the air. If there isn't enough to fill my rolled up piece of notebook paper, I use some of the tobacco from the Dutch Master cigars they empty on the table for the outer shell. As if my chest isn't already on fire, I take a puff and swallow the smoke. I have to finish my first blunt, despite how light-headed I am. My aunt, Shontee Vonzella Douglas—with no meaning for her first or middle name, which could be the reason she suffered most—knows of none of this. No one does.

The house seems vacant on the weekends. I become a single father of three to my little cousins because Shontee works crazy hours. Her boyfriend and his acquaintances are too busy getting high and drunk, bagging up, or having sex to care what is going on with her children and me. The money from transporting drugs exceeds all the money I ever made combined. It's daunting, but the payoff surely comforts me. Once Shontee realizes my motive for visiting during the weekends, she bans me from babysitting and coming to visit altogether.

I love Shontee even though we don't have much of an auntienephew relationship. She is much closer with Sista. Shontee is always working, which is why I am soon babysitting during the week too. As much as I wish we did have an in-depth bond, she cries too much for us to ever engage one another when she is home. But there is a mutual respect between us for the struggles we both face. It was my Uncle Antoine who was killed but he was her brother; her sister, Poncella, was my mother—her mother, Mary, was my Grandma. It is as if we fear growing too close to one another to avoid the mental and emotional destruction one of us will face when the curse strikes again. So I understand why she forbids me from visiting. But I have other things on my mind.

As I plot to sneak over and take a couple of packs up to Lorraine while she is out, the house is raided with me standing at the end of the block. Before I take off, I see my precious little cousins get carried out by those same blue uniformed devils that took me away from the house just two blocks away in Waverly. Miraculously, they return to Shontee's custody. The raids continue for some time, though. It becomes an all-too-familiar part of their lives. Soon, but not soon enough, Shontee grows tired of it and the traumatic effect it has on her children and makes provision to remove her family from that dead-end street and situation.

With a new house aligned, Shontee decides to leave her boyfriend. When she tells him, according to the testimony of her oldest son Daquan, the two fight both verbally and physically. She walks to the phone booth to call the police when her boyfriend grabs his .357 magnum from behind the back door and walks up the alley to meet her. Daquan runs up the street after his mother and sees her boyfriend shoot her on the corner of Greenmount Avenue and East 27th Street. He stays with his mother until the ambulance comes almost thirty minutes later.

Shontee arrives at the hospital brain dead and fights for her life with the help of machines. She is so determined not to let the curse break her. It is when I see her in this vegetated state that she shows the greatest strength.

The doctors say she can't hear us, but I know she can because every day, I whisper in her ear, "Fight it!" and she does. She knows the "it" I speak of.

The family decides to take her off the machines that are

her only weapons to fight, and she continues without them. For ten minutes, she brawls and battles, refusing to give in. I am well pleased. In my eyes, the curse doesn't defeat her. She just grows tired of fighting it. Returning home, I pick up a gun for the first time. Unsure of whom to use it on—him or myself—I refrain from both options for my little cousins, specifically Daquan, who witnessed it all. He lived with his mom his entire life and watched her be murdered. That's much worse than hearing of the death of an estranged mother as I did. I can't imagine the pain he feels.

I am now left alone underneath the weight of the curse. Robert Arthur Douglas—bright fame as strong as a bear in dark waters. Mom giving me her last name births me into this curse, yet giving me the first and middle names of my father declares me to be great and hopefully strong enough to overpower these dark waters. I have indeed grown accustomed to the tactics of the force behind it, so I aim to curse this curse, break this curse, and destroy that which consumed my family. The fact that every suicidal and homicidal attempt has been unsuccessful is hell within itself. As of now, I have avoided it, but I feel dead without them. All of those surrounding me were taken so easily and I, being the one who prayed that my life would end, remain. Even when I think God is taking too long, I attempt it myself but I am saved by my all-time hero. And as much as I hate to admit it, something supernatural spares me from the three people who make unsuccessful attempts on my life too.

I am still standing. I am still strong.

My Favorite Tie

IT WAS A VERY NICE tie, which was given to me; to wear to the funeral of my mother to-be.

It looked so nice and hid the pain well, but my countenance fell, and my heart lost morale.

That same tie I wore, to usher her into the dirt, was the same tie that almost erased all the hurt.

The next time I tied it, I had death on my head, because the other end I tied to the top of the bunked bed.

Not thinking ahead, I jumped on down and hung there awhile, not making a sound.

After a while, the breaths began to cease, when all of a sudden the tie was released.

Desperately hoping that my life was now over, I was lifted from the floor and placed on his shoulders.

Breathing in my mouth, I began to cough.

When it was then I realized, I wasn't dead after all.

A Brother Unkept

"And the Lord said unto Cain, 'Where is Abel thy brother?' And he said,
'I know not: am I my brother's keeper?'"
–Genesis 4:9

I'M SUPPOSED TO BE MY brother's keeper, but I left my brother unkept. Yet it is my brother's keeping of me that keeps me here today. His hands are the ones that release the knot to my favorite tie, causing me to fall to the ground. It is his shoulders he places me on and his breath breathed into my lungs. The late Daniel Joshua Bowser Junior is my brother—the keeper of me.

Even though Danny and I are not biological brothers, we fight like brothers, we fight others like brothers, and we challenge one another like brothers. Like a younger brother, I mimic his every move, but he encourages me to approach life's obstacles more objectively and responsibly to produce more positive results.

Due to the excessive fighting and bickering between the two of us, people often misunderstand our relationship. Ma doesn't. In fact, she can't understand why he, being four years older than me, only receives the advice I offer in crucial situations.

Oddly enough, the only thing we never fight over is our

personal space. We share rooms. The last one we shared had wooden panels as walls. I can't remember the floor because I only saw it twice— move-in day and the day we moved out. The lapsed time had cleaned clothes, shoes, paper, dirty underwear, socks, towels, wash cloths, dirt, video games, my stuffed animals, dirty sheets, dirty clothes, coats, hats, gloves, drum sticks, basketballs, toys and other random items covering the floor. But we knew where everything was. And when someone entered our room in our absence, we knew. We tried cleaning it once, but there were huge roaches living underneath our worldly possessions. These roaches were monsters. They were specially bred because they ran with lightning speed. If they felt threatened enough, they mounted up on their wings and flew to the ceiling. We couldn't get them down and I had to sleep on the top bunk. Danny wouldn't let me sleep with him. We were some dirty little boys—still are. No one can really understand us or understand why we choose to live this way. But we can relate to each other as hard as it is for others to relate to us, which is what solemnizes our brotherhood.

For the first ten years though, he despises me because before I come to live with them, he is the baby boy. Now he is the neglected middle child who has nothing to call his own, not even his life.

Whenever I get him into trouble, he asks bitterly, "Why don't you go live with your own family?" Before I can answer, he does, "Oh, I forgot. They don't want you." It never really hurt me until I found out the truth about my real parents.

As if that isn't enough torment, Danny sometimes grabs my head and sprays his flatulence into my face or ear to further torture me. He doesn't need a reason for anything. While I slept once, he cut patches of hair out of my four puff balls. Everyone at school had jokes. But what I hate most is that he is chubby—for two reasons. He shoves his man boob in my mouth because he thinks I act like a baby and assumes it his duty to breastfeed me. Once I tried to bite it off, so he settles for rubbing his sweaty, hairy armpits on my lips "because they are chapped." Two, I hate his belly button. It is a never ending cave. When his chest is bare, his nipples look like eyes, that narrow streak of blond hair forms the nose, and the navel resembles a mouth that always wears the same expression. He feeds it too, which drives me insane. That's his only motivation to do so. He stuffs cotton, crackers, and anything else he can find to fit in that hole. He leaves it in for days at a time and induces the vomiting of this "thing" until the now foreign object and its horrific scent falls on my face. I don't know if I dislike him or it more.

"Ma!" I scream at the top of my lungs.

She rarely answers these calls from either of us because she knows their nature. So, I chase him with the metal ladder to our bunked beds or any blunt object that shows him I am serious.

"Ma, Lil' Rob crazy," he somehow manages to spew out over top of his laughter as he runs.

There is a major turnabout in our relationship when my real mom dies. We grow very close, but not to the point that I can fully understand him. Many of his ways are too enigmatic for anyone to comprehend. Like the time he comes home from the club after being jumped. His light-skinned face is accented by black and purple rings around his one open eye and the other that is swelled shut. His tall stature is stunted due to the dramatic limp in his walk. I suppose it is related to the rip in his jeans that shows the blood leaking from his knee. Half of his dreadlocks are pulled out of the left side of his head and his back spills more blood from the various stab wounds he suffers from that night as well. As he stumbles to the mirror, to assess the damage, he screams, "Man! They chipped my tooth! Girls love my teeth!" We stare at him, trying not to laugh, but his laughter conveniently ushers ours in.

Only he could turn such a tragedy into a laughing moment. Like us lying in the dark with no electricity and a refrigerator full of spoiled food as he serves as entertainment for the entire house for hours constantly shouting his favorite line from Mad T.V., "Me sooo horny."

But outside of his sense of humor and his outlook on life, I will never understand why he regards me in such a way. He endures jail for me and many other unwarranted punishments. He keeps me from seeing the juvenile detention center at too young of an age when I intentionally bust the window of a car that he falsely confesses to. When I begin to act out in school to ward off the bullies, he beats me to a bloody pulp until he knows the truth as to why I act out, which is the same tactic he uses with the bullies. The fear and respect he instills in me keeps me off the streets during school hours, hours after curfew, or anytime he is around.

Ranging from the drum set to the basketball court—especially on the basketball court—and everything in between, Danny has skills. He is the type of person I envy, the type that masters anything he puts his hands to in a short matter of time. To me he is a genius. Not just because he possesses this gift but he also receives two offers to skip a grade because his teachers and counselors view him as both academically and behaviorally mature. He is surely destined for greatness. But five wrong words, which are simple to me, turn his life upside down and there is nothing I can say or do to convince him to climb out of the slump he falls in.

"You don't understand, Lil Rob. I don't expect you to," he sulks.

For the first fifteen years of his life, he hears how much he looks, acts and even smells like his father. What once serves as a compliment is now nothing but a complete insult. Danny thinks I can't identify with him in his crisis because Big Danny, his father, is in and out of his life. Maybe he is right. Big Danny comes to live with us periodically. He also disappears on occasion too. Luckily for Danny, Big Danny experiences more lows in his life than highs, so he is around more often than not—physically. Regardless, Danny looks up to him and aspires to be the best on the basketball court, in the classroom, and underneath the hood of his father's car whenever Big Danny is around. I try calling him Daddy too, like Danny, but Ma and Danny both nip that in the bud. I don't know why I want to. He does nothing for me. Nor does he take me anywhere other than to do donuts in the middle of the street in his black Mazda, which is the greatest adventure of my childhood. Oh, and to the flea market to serve Danny.

Danny runs Big Danny's tables at the flea market. I am his assistant. He is quite the business man. I, on the other hand, can't sell a banana to an ape. He has both charisma and a sure future in sales if his basketball dream falls through. I doubt it will, though. Big Danny is always surprised at the amount of money Danny reels in through bargaining with customers. His father's encouragement, approving smile and occassional stroke on the head is Danny's sole motivation in everything he does. But five words heard from the courtroom change the course of Danny's life when Ma requests a portion of child support to be paid by Big Danny. The judge grants Ma's reasonable request.

The next words spoken damage Danny to the core and soon lead him astray, "I...need...a...DNA...test," Big Danny demands. He didn't need one at birth or when he comes to mooch off Ma, but he does now. When the judge orders Big Danny to be a good and real man, he stoops to the lowest low to shuck his fatherly duties. Danny's eyes dim and his face grows grim as his eyes feast on the one he once admired.

The entire day you can tell Danny is furious but he refuses to eat or speak. He just leaves the house.

Ma runs behind him, "Danny, where are you going?" She receives no reply. "Ten o'clock," is all she yells to his silence.

He misses curfew. Ma figures he ran away so she calls the local authorities to file a missing persons report, only to hear that Danny is in their custody. He is detained for assaulting a pizza man and bears an additional charge for malicious destruction. Big Danny and Ma go to pick him up from the juvenile detention center and as Big Danny tries disciplining him, Danny fights back.

"That boy is strong," is all I hear Big Danny utter as he walks to his car covering the cuts and bruises.

After days of complete silence, at two o'clock in the morning, Danny lifts my bed on the top bunk with his feet for me to fall over the bars and onto the floor. It is about a six foot drop. Luckily, the floor is cushioned by all our clothing, with the exception of random toys I sometimes land on. This, which normally enrages me, somehow pleases me because it is normal behavior.

I have to retaliate somehow, but before I do, I hear through his shaky voice and tears, "I would never do that to my son. I'm nothing like him!"

I don't know how to reply. So, I just sit up with him.

Finally I mumble, "Yo, let's play Nintendo."

Shortly after his first arrest comes another for smoking marijuana. Then it's possession of marijuana and other narcotics with the intent to distribute—next, the gun charges. School, he leaves. Basketball, he no longer has time for. His time and energy are invested into the streets, girls, and money. His repressed anger, he invests in violent crime.

"Danny, you can't let this stop you, yo. You have to keep it moving," was all I could offer.

"You don't understand, Lil Rob. I don't expect you to."

In due time, Danny abandons the street life when his girlfriend directs his attention to the seed growing in her womb. Immediately, he makes the decision to create a better life for his family. He gives up the violent acts of the streets and relocates to a neighboring area with his girlfriend and her family. But he moves on a street where drug trafficking is still a major issue. It's not easy to escape the presence of such in this city. He requests that the local drug dealers not peddle their product from his front step when an altercation breaks out, ending in my brother lying on the curb bleeding out. One of his friends that instigated the situation was strapped, but fled the scene and the state when the shots broke out—leaving Danny alone and unarmed. He is shot twice: once in the back, about an inch away from the spine, and in the back of the neck. He bleeds on the curb for forty minutes before the ambulance arrives. The station is only three blocks away from the crime scene.

Danny loses his life on the ninth of August, 2004. There is nothing I can do to keep him from this. At fifteen years old, the seed of the agony sown into my life brought about the monster within me because of this.

For the first time God speaks to me, the day prior to the incident, in a dream. Not every dream is from God. This one is.

We walk into beautiful green trees and colorful fruits that the sun shines graciously upon—neither of us know where we are headed. My brother begins to talk about how tired he's become. He says he finally needs rest. I've never heard those words from him before because he never shows any signs of fatigue. Before I can reply, we are standing before an enormous white house. The sounds coming from within are of pure bliss and ecstasy. No music is playing but the house booms with many voices and of much laughter. We are now surrounded by people we don't know, who don't know each another, when a fair woman steps out of the mansion and calls for everyone to come in. The crowd, including my brother, rushes to the door instantaneously, but I am forbidden to go in. I insist on following the crowd but the door slams in my face before I can get a glimpse inside. Turning to see who remains, I realize I am left alone in this strange land. I grow afraid, so I wait. He never comes out. I sit wailing in the dark as I listen to those inside rejoice.

When I awake from the dream, nothing makes sense until around three o'clock p.m. two days later when Ma breaks the news that Daniel Joshua Bowser Junior, her only son and my brother, was killed the night before. I make a conscious yet failing effort to sound taken aback. Now my dream makes sense. He and the rest of the crowd were going to live in that mansion on that day and I was left alone in this dark, cold world while they enjoy the festive life within those four walls.

Left unkept for just one night, I almost lose my life. The details must be withheld, but I face a physical death from the point blank range of a 9-mm handgun and the possibility of permanently residing in the annex of the Maryland House of Correction for using this .40 caliber one that stands fully loaded. Mine is aimed at another. I am ready for either result—one more than the other— but this time I am willing to take my chances because if justice isn't impartial, I may not spend the rest of my life in prison. My brother's murderer isn't. In fact, he is due to be released soon. The defense attorney had the audacity to stand before a judge at the trial to ask that a lesser sentence be offered to the defendant because the details of that night were too inconclusive to adequately explain why the shooting took place. Because of my brother's prior criminal record and the fact that drugs were found near his dead body, it was permitted. Also, because the dead cannot defend themselves, the defendant receives a sentence of five years in prison. The prosecutor does not contest.

This makes me regret that things didn't work in my favor that one night because if I were arrested, I could always cite this case to plea a lesser sentence. But with my luck and the curse in pursuit, the courts would bury me alive.

Every night after the first, I have the same dream as before with a different setting each time. He is alive and we have a little more time together. Every morning, I arise disappointed. To end the sobs, I don't sleep, to avoid the torture. Of all the dreams, the last is of most importance. It assuages a very burdening issue concerning his residence in his afterlife.

"Clean my room, Lil Rob. Lil Rob, clean my room," he continually repeats.

I refuse. We had separate rooms in Ma's new house, but they were still kept the same—filthy. Cleaning his room will require days of work. But I awaken and do just that. Unbeknownst to me, I am cleaning with a purpose. I find lots of items that I hold as memorabilia today, even the item that puts Ma and me at peace with his death. He was never baptized but believed in Jesus, yet never confessed Him as his personal Savior. It is a tract that I find. On the back, there is a place for those who believe in Christ and confess Him as their personal Lord and Savior to fill out and mail it in. He filled it out, but was not afforded the opportunity to mail it. My soul rejoices. I am pleased to know that his soul is not sentenced to burn in hell for eternity. He was baptized by God's spirit even though he never made it to the baptismal pool. God finally grants me some closure in one aspect of my life.

When I show Ma the tract, she screeches with a boisterous,

never ending cry. She even reads it at his funeral. I read the biography in the obituary, which is as difficult as it was to write and design. I finally act as his keeper by doing his obituary its full justice. I can't risk someone doing the same type of job as on Mom's obituary. Plus, besides Ma, I knew him best. I add this short poem that I wrote for him to it:

The Two of Us

The two of us shared most of our lives, say it isn't so.

You were with me through my highs, and helped me when I'm low.

Just to watch you struggle would always help me grow.

We spent our time together, and these few things are true.

We always fussed, we'd always fight, we laughed and cried the blues.

But you were always there for me and I was there for you.

So when the struggle was really rough, we always stuck it through.

But this is not enough. I have to honor him for the way he kept me. I owe it to him.

Knowing the family struggles with the funeral costs due to his lack of life insurance, I contribute the money I made from a summer job along with other funds I accumulated, but it isn't sufficient. As fate would have it, I come across a lady affiliated with the program I work for (The Baltimore Algebra Project) who lost both her husband and her son in the month of August. It is a custom of hers to help those in need in this particular month. We both share the same level of pain in many ways and can relate to one another.

To my surprise, she writes a check for almost ten thousand dollars to pay the funeral costs of my brother. It isn't my money, but if I never encountered that woman, his funeral may have been just a memorial over his ashes. God places me in a position to give my brother a proper burial. I know that I now owe Him—God. I just don't know what the debt is to repay.

Even though I couldn't serve as his keeper on earth, I kept him in his death and keep him in my heart today. Brothers for life.

Broken Covenant

"But I have promises to keep. And miles to go before I sleep." -Robert Frost

MY BROTHER WAS TWENTY YEARS old when he was killed. But I doubt he has rested any and I'm the cause of this restlessness.

The book of I Samuel tells the story of David and Jonathan growing to identify one another as brothers, despite their genetic origins—like Danny and I. Jonathan, sensing that his end is approaching, urges David to promise to show kindness to Jonathan's descendants by providing their needs in his absence. David complies and is held accountable before God and Jonathan to uphold this covenant. Fortunately, he fulfills his promise in the book of II Samuel when he is anointed king of Israel after Jonathan's death. Being the younger of the two, yet mentally and spiritually stronger, David does not allow his covenant to be broken. I'm sorry I can't say the same for myself.

If a man makes a vow to the LORD, or takes an oath to bind himself with a binding obligation, he shall not violate his word; he shall do according

to all that proceeds out of his mouth.
–Number 30:2

You shall be careful to perform what goes out from your lips, just as you have voluntarily vowed to the LORD your God, what you have promised.
–Deuteronomy 23:23

When you make a vow to God, do not be late in paying it, for He takes no delight in fools, Pay what you vow!
–Ecclesiastes 5:4

Again, you have heard that the ancients were told, 'You shall not make false vows, but shall fulfill your vows to the LORD.' But I say to you, make no oath at all, either by heaven, for it is the throne of God, or by the earth, for it is the footstool of His feet, or by Jerusalem, for it is the city of the Great King. Nor shall you make an oath by your head, for you cannot make one hair white or black. But let your statement be, 'Yes, yes' or 'No, no'; anything beyond these is of evil.
–Matthew 5:33–37

There you have it.

Whether you swear on God's name or even promise on the strength of your own, God holds you personally accountable. The fulfillment of David's promise allows Jonathan to rest peacefully in his grave but I now face judgment before God because I have yet to honor my brother's dying requests.

Everyone is born with a purpose. I assume that after it is fulfilled, life soon ends. I am charged to care for and show kindness to the fruition of my brother's purpose. He receives the news of his first and only child being formed in the womb and is killed one week later. After receiving the news, he tells me of his child and how he seeks to be a true example and good leader for his family. Just as Jonathan urges David, he urges me to vow that I will always care for and protect his child in the event he is unable to. He must've realized that his purpose was complete and his confrontation with death was near. I readily take on the responsibility because I do not expect him to depart this life at age twenty. Five days after I vow to care for what we later find out to be a baby girl, his allotted time runs out.

De'Asia Angelica Bowser, the beat of my heart, the only piece of the one who saved me, and the one I dedicate my life to, enters the world on April 5th, 2005. I celebrate her life and thank God for her because without her, life would now have no meaning. For God to create one person, my brother, for the sole purpose of joining with another individual, his girlfriend, to create another being, my niece, is potent. And I, Robert Arthur Douglas—neither monster nor minister—am charged to guard this investment of life. From April of 2005 to August of 2005, I act on this promise, but have left it undone ever since.

De'Asia is born the most beautiful person my eyes ever rest on. Instantly, she is the joy of my world and new hope for living. Her presence alone soothes the malice of the monster. She has a spirit that leaps inside of her so much so, that it causes others to be aroused by her mere presence. Her smile brightens my day and tears me apart simultaneously.

I see him in every ounce of her.

I fear that one day she will go to school and see the fathers of all the other kids and be intrigued to inquire about hers. My only thought in shielding her from this is to send her to an urban innercity public school where only the minorities have fathers.

She spends every weekend with us and occasionally time during the week too. By the end of May, she is living with us permanently because her mother drops her off and doesn't return.

For three months there is no sign of her. Maybe Danny foresaw this abandonment, which is why he charges me with this task. Love isn't strong enough to describe the rhythm in my heart that has her name scribed all over it. I give her what I can without anyone discovering that I too now have resorted to the street life. I hold her for what seems like forever and laugh at those gums she loves to show me. It's as if she is my own. She is now.

Ma then seeks out government assistance for De'Asia since there is no sign of her mother. The courts track her down to address the matter and she claims that we will not allow her to pick up De'Asia. One day, she returns for De'Asia as if it is the end of her normal weekend visit. She is very pleasant and somewhat loopy—no apology or explanation at all.

Her parting words are, "De'Asia, say see you next weekend!" smiling. Once they part, she refuses to allow us to see the baby again. The end of that August was the last time I saw De'Asia—go figure.

I find out her mother now involves herself intimately with a former friend of my brother, which is the underlying reason for me being unable to see my niece. It also explains her disappearance. Today, it has been three years. If I were to see De'Asia tomorrow, she would have no idea who I am. So I live with the pain of my brother being disgusted with me. He's finally reached a place in life where he can be at peace, but my unfaithfulness does not permit it. His life's purpose, De'Asia, is now subjected to the hands of a malicious idiot and so-called friend who almost cost me my license to preach because of an altercation between the two of us that ended violently.

I locate their home. I just want to see my niece, so I humbly make this known as De'Asia's mom tells me from the window to go away.

The boyfriend opens the door to say, "Get the hell off my

front before I whip your ass."

From the window I hear De'Asia call him dad. She's requesting for him to come back in. I'd recognize that voice anywhere. It's embedded in my heart. Her pitch, tone and swift speech all resemble her smooth-talking father, her real father. The monster reacts at full force. I yank the screen door open, breaking the lock he hides behind, and drag him to the street behind my car. I don't want De'Asia to witness what I prepare to do. I hurt the rear bumper of my car with his head by bashing it repeatedly. He's bleeding, so I let him go. Everyone knows not to touch a fiend's blood. Contemplating running him over, I hear sirens and flee the scene. During this altercation, an associate minister at my church calls me and hears the obscenities that I wouldn't dare shout from the pulpit.

None of that matters to me. All I want is a fair chance to fulfill my promise to my brother so that I won't face judgment for it later and his disappointment in me now.

No Beauty, Just Beast

"It is because every one under Heaven recognizes beauty as beauty, that the idea of ugliness exists. And equally if every one recognized virtue as virtue, this would merely create fresh conceptions of wickedness."
-Tao Te Ching

NO BEAUTY INHABITS THIS BEASTLY creature or the actions it takes to feel a sense of self-gratification. All innocence and emotional attachments to anything or anyone are severed completely at this point because of the events of Augusts. August birthed me to kill me by taking me away from Mom. Then it takes Mom away from me only to later take my younger siblings too. August took Danny. August was the last I saw of De'Asia.

The monstrous acts of destroying lives—one mother, father, and child at a time—are the affects its actions have brought on the world in living this street life. But I was not alone in any of these deeds, which was my first mistake.

I start out at an entry-level position, a transporter. After a few short months, I am promoted to a corner boy.

The question many people dare to ask me is, "How can you do to someone else's mother what someone once did to yours?"

I don't care anymore! My reply is, "If they don't get it from me, they'll walk down the block to get it from somebody else."

I mean it. That nonchalant demeanor is the reason for my success in the game, but more so for my failures in life. Perusing the street corners, I build my own empire and fortify it with walls that eventually collapse.

I thought of Rick the other night. I often do. I wonder if he is still alive. Even though I run the risk of him wanting to kill me, I go to his last known strip to find him because I owe him. Rick was my first running partner.

At thirteen, we pick up our first packs and establish our territory in Southeast Baltimore. Unlike most that are new to the game and start with marijuana, Rick and I hit the streets hard with crackcocaine. We are two hungry young thugs who grow tired of the struggles of the hood. We loathe living poorly and going without. It didn't bother us until now though because we weren't exposed to environments differing vastly from ours before this year. On our school field trips, we pass by communities with trees, grass, maintained public gardens and homes with space between them. There are basketball goals in the driveways and back yards of these houses. In our hoods, we play on milk crates nailed to telephone poles. Life now has contrast. So does the world, we just never knew it. We can now examine the visible lines of poor and rich, peace and calamity, pretty and ugly, concrete and grass but we never see color until we experiment with the drug game. Whites are people and blacks are people, all equal. Those issues of injustice are things of the past. We think this because there aren't whites in our areas to oppress and govern us. They only travel here to buy our drugs and leave. It's too violent here, where blacks kill one another every day. Hispanics are moving in rapidly, creating a territorial war between us and them.

The whites come to buy cocaine; the blacks use crack as do the Hispanics. The whites don't go near crack. This isn't racial judgment on our behalf, simply observation. Rick and I push pure cocaine too for our particular demographic that demands it. We, in the hood, call it "that white boy." Crack, we call "ready rock." We see color as differences only, no one better than the other—like male and female. Each group just has different preferences. That's until we are the victims of hate.

It happens on the corner of Eastern Avenue and Highland Avenue in Highlandtown, right outside of the Enoch Pratt Free Library where a white couple sits on the bus stop bench. They are high, dirty, and dressed in all black. The guy has a shaved head. Rick and I are coming from school, headed to the block to push our rock.

The guy on the bench spots us and says, "Well, look at these niggers here. Where do you think you're going, nigger?"

He pulls out a long, thick silver chain and swings it in the air— gesturing that he plans to hit us with it. The woman who is with him follows suit with her own chain. I panic and pick up a rock because I am pinned between the library and the bridal shop next door. The woman swings at Rick but misses and he punches her in the face. Rick is a very heavy fellow, and heavy handed too. He is the one who chipped my tooth when we were rough housing. Needless to say, she falls. The guy turns to her and back to me, angrily. He comes charging. I throw the rock right in his face as hard as I can and it connects. Hitting him physically would do nothing. I only weigh 75 lbs. He hits the ground. Only she is moving. Rick and I run.

Before this, I didn't care about color. Now I see that some things are still black and white with some people, just like Grandma said. I don't hate white people because of this, but I wanted to. Then again, I would be a hypocrite as I grow furious when whites cast judgments on the entire black race for the actions of a few people. Plus, whites are the base of my clientele. My teachers are white.

My employer at the job I worked before hustling is white. He was generous enough to employ me.

Child labor laws state that I cannot legally work at age eleven, but it is my first part-time position at 30 hours a week for five dollars an hour at a local fishing tackle shop. Ma can't afford the materials I need to attend my magnet middle school, so I need my own means to purchase new uniforms and supplies. I also contribute to household expenses, so we all suffer when I am fired for lying about my age two years later. My love for school and pain from struggling to keep food in the house forces me to make a way.

Black, who already assumed his position in the streets, and Rick are the only two I keep in my camp. You can't trust many in this game. I trust Rick because we grew up together. Black puts me on with his connect and that risk of his reputation helps me to build trust in him. Rick has his own connect. When Black's connect and I finally trust one another enough to do business, he fronts me a pack. Black gets locked up. I'm now his number one hustler. Rick and I hold down a strip that we aren't familiar with, so no one would move in on Black's territory, in addition to our own. But I live on the sound principles of M.O.E.—Money Over Everything—which makes it all worthwhile.

Whatever it takes, I am determined to get what I need!

I hear a lot of how the game turns people sour and ruthless from the O.G.'s that remain in the streets. That isn't my experience initially. However, new means become necessary to get what I need. Black's connect is pimping me with a 70/30 deal (seventy percent of the money earned is returned to the connect, leaving me with the remaining thirty percent), so I devise a plan that will drastically increase my income and keep his constant. But one day when Rick and I close shop, we are robbed by stick-up boys. They know where I keep my stash—Rick doesn't even know where I keep it. Prior to this, I paid my connect and randomly thought to put all of my money in my back left pocket: I use each pocket for different bills to avoid pulling all of it out at once. As our knees buckle at gun point, they search everywhere except that lucky back left pocket. They take Rick's money and drugs, though, including his connect's money. Rick cries.

"Yo, man up," I yell at him as we run away from the barrel of the gun aimed at our backs.

Rick is on a 60/40 deal. As we catch our breath in his backyard, his connect calls and wants either his money or his drugs tonight. I'm not giving him any of mine. When I vowed M.O.E., I meant it. That night, Rick disappears. My guilt causes me to worry until I spot him six months later on my way to the west side. I want to turn around but I don't know how he feels about me not helping him and I don't know the reason he relocated. So I keep it moving. My love for money grows greater than my love for those who risk their lives with me. I could see then that in this game, you have no friends. I couldn't be the friend I desired when it came to sacrificing for one another. Regretfully, it took worse for me to learn that.

I keep the establishment moving and operate as a sole proprietor in this business. I make even more money with all of the clients dependent on me. I don't desire another partner, but my connect insists I replace Rick with Duke. Duke soon crosses me. Then, my connect cuts me off for crossing him. In light of the fact that he used me for this long and provided no opportunities for advancement, I was insatiably thirsty which amplified the hunger that already existed.

Trying to help Duke earn more than the one-hundred dollars a week he averages, I tell him my secret on manipulating the product we sell to make more money than our connect. I figure he too should be adequately compensated for the risks taken, but he chooses to advance by crossing me by snitching. They take me into an abandoned house and beat my body into submission. I suppose it is embarrassing to be outwitted by someone more than half your age with not nearly as much street cred. However, Dough, another connect, admires my hustle and fearless schemes enough to front me a pack on a 55/45 deal that introduces me to the dope game. When one door closes, another one opens.

I make enough money off my first dope pack to front my own pack in the crack game. I continue as a dope boy though even though it is riskier. Selling dope is a different game. I get robbed by too many fiends, stick-up boys, drug dealers, friends, and foes until I grow tired. So, I start running with Pablo. We explore new monetary schemes.

We partner in our hustle and rob people too. Only fifteen years old, we don't have the audacity to rob the older drugs dealers, but we rob the younger ones that work for them and the wealthy people of the neighborhood (or what we consider wealthy) instead. I see why I was robbed so many times. I can't be mad at the stick-up boys or anyone else because the money that it returns is so plentiful and easy. Regardless, "Ain't no money like dope money." Our eagerness and zeal soon creates conflict because we start robbing too close to home. We target an older guy living one block away because he is flashy, so it's to teach him a lesson. He is the only one ever to take a stand against us by showing up at Pablo's doorstep with the police. He points Pablo out and claims I played no part in the robbery. I had the gun. It was only a B.B. gun. Pablo glances at me as they shove his head down into the patrol car, and I stand carelessly as I go free. Again, my love for money and self is more transparent. I stare at every piece of U.S. currency I toil to earn as it reads, "In God we trust." The money is my god. That is the only thing trustworthy enough to deserve my faithfulness. If I do what I need, it will always be there to take me to the next level—what a mockery.

With Pablo incarcerated, Black is released and arrested again after he finds out who was robbing me. I still don't know how he found out. I don't know who it was, still. Black thinks it to be his personal responsibility to protect me. He also finds it to be his duty to tell Ma of the life I am living. He says it is for my own good and that I am in way too deep now. His going back to jail after that pleases me. Ma comes to the stash house and drags me home.

But not even she can kill the monster in me. Get money!

Pablo forgives me after his release and we continue in the building of our empire of burning junkies, robbing, stealing, and breaking and entering, but I know he can't trust me. I can't trust me. We proceed with our lives, but first we have to recover from the beatings we take from his brothers the day Pablo came home.

It's not just about money anymore. Now in the game, everyone is seeking power and respect too. Now, if you cross over into certain territories you don't get dirty looks anymore, but bullets flying and breathing down your neck. Now you need a gun for protection because your clique is no longer enough. At the age of sixteen, the streets just got real, and I want out.

It's August. My seventeenth birthday is in one week, senior year is starting, and I just started a job at Pizza Hut. I'm accustomed to making at least one hundred dollars in a single hour, but these six bucks and fifteen cents will suffice for now—anything to escape the dangers of the streets. I never intended to live the street life forever, so it is best to adjust now while I am able. I no longer work for anyone, but front my own packs of dope and cocaine. So I owe no one any money. My escape route is paved for me.

I didn't have a birthday party—I never do. No one has ever made a big deal out of the day, not even me. But the fact that the normal tragic patterns of August have been assuaged this year is enough to celebrate. Turning seventeen creates a hope that life will soon begin to progress in a positive direction. I just have to make it through this one last day—the thirty-first—until I'm safe for sure.

I work a twelve hour shift prepping, making, cutting and selling pizza, breadsticks and all that compliments the two. It ends smoothly with two hours remaining in the day. If I miss the last bus, I will be standing outside until morning, so I ask my coworker, Josh, for a ride home.

"Yea, yo, I got you," is his reply.

As tired as I am, I am not in a rush to get home. Things have only gotten progressively worse there with Danny gone and De'Asia absent from our lives. Normally, I serve as Ma's outlet to release any built up tension. In the past, the slightest typical adolescent behavior out of me lands me in the Social Services' office with Ma telling the case manager how tired she is of me and that she refuses to take care of me any longer. Each time, they bribe her with money to take me home. She complies with the increase. Sometimes, I wish they would place me elsewhere because I start to feel like a pawn to control the government and pressure them into meeting her requests. I can't understand why I am still working if she is constantly receiving money for me. I love her and I feel like she loves me too, maybe she just doesn't want me anymore. Still, none of the step-child treatment was as unbearable as now—it's to the point I'm tempted to lash back at her.

Josh and I pull up at my house with his step-father driving. The dashboard reads 11:50 p.m. I get out and approach the steps. They are waiting for me to enter the house but I signal his step-father to pull off and he does. Searching my pockets for my keys, I realize they must've fallen out in the car. I dare not tell Ma that. I have two choices, knock or sleep on the porch. I'm just going to sleep here because I know there will be a struggle to get in. It isn't the first

I've done so. As I sit on the cold, stone porch, the door opens.

11:58 p.m.

"Where is your keys?" Ma asks.

I hurry to brush past her before answering as if I left them upstairs. Normally, she is asleep by now. She must've been waiting for me to get in.

Approaching the steps, I say, "I think I left them at work."

"Fine place for them, Dodo."

I fight to ignore her. I have a temper, and things can only grow ugly from here. They have done so in the past.

11:59 p.m.

"You know what, I'm sick of your disrespect and your hatefulness!" she carries on. She rants on about how tired of me and my crazy self she is. I prepare for my shower to get the smell of pepperoni off me and to avoid any escalation of the matter. "You're just like your damn mother!" is how she chooses to end her speech.

I snap.

I trash the bedroom to keep from assaulting her for this insult. She always talks about my mother. I hate it. I am used to other insults and being treated as the ugly step-child, but since Danny's passing, any positive advancement I make in life becomes an opportunity for punishment. I think it is because senior year will be over soon. Everyone swore I wouldn't finish, even she. So she has to prevent it in some way. Danny didn't finish school, neither did her daughter. She wishes what happened to him happened to me instead. In ways, we share that common interest.

"Get your stuff and get out, now!" she comes charging up the stairs. I ask her where I am to go at this time of night but she shows no regard.

The china house in Patterson Park is where I sleep. It's dark enough for me to go unnoticed because I'm positive Ma called the police, but enough light to defend myself properly if need be. I pack heat for protection because around these parts, one of the most common pastimes is beating up and robbing the homeless. On occasion, I stay with Black's sister and her kids, but they have roaches. No other animal terrifies me like roaches. Plus, I am too prideful to admit my homeless state to anyone. So I stay as much as I can bear and for as long as I can go undetected.

I still have to eat. I need clothes too. I get into a fight at Pizza Hut with a fellow employee, so they fire me. With no other options, I have to accept a pack I am fronted by Dough, again.

My last year of high school continues and by the start of last period one day, everyone is expecting a laugh out of me. They are confused by this new temperament. This past summer changed me. None of my classmates know this fire breathing monster. The class clown from the past three years is replaced with a stern, scrunched up face thug—a lot like Grandma's face. There is nothing to laugh at. I can't smile. I can't even smirk. Nothing is funny. I stink. Once I shower in the locker room, I have to find a place in the park.

Robert A. Douglas

The Intervention

A double minded man is unstable in all his ways.
–James 1:8

Addictions

"Every man must decide whether he will walk in the light of creative altruism or in the darkness of destructive selfishness."
-Dr. Martin Luther King, Jr.

Despite popular belief, my addiction to money and facing the detriment it brings isn't my greatest quandary. I've suffered it the longest, but once I made the decision to never relapse again, I stick to it. Abusing drugs is recreational, to test the product I purchase. I learn from the experiments of others not to make it a habit. Plus, I can't chance getting high off my own supply; it can be costly. Alcohol is never the slightest struggle until recently. It starts with a sip of wine occasionally and evolves into entire bottles of vodka being devoured several times in a week. Still, my high blood alcohol levels fall far from topping the charts.

My one true vice, my uncontrollable addiction, that insatiable craving is to the female species—the greatest to overcome.

Forty-five seconds of my teenage life causes this. Not even a full minute goes by before my virginity is gone and the experience concludes, but my love for the words I hear remains.

"You done?" she questions the brief encounter.

No, those are not the words. Embarrassed, I lie, "No girl. I'm just taking this condom off."

Lying has become a fond habit. Regardless, I love every millisecond of the experience. Not the sex itself. My hormones aren't raging that much. I don't get any attention from girls. They are attracted to the money and the lifestyle that a hustler lives, but I'm the boy they don't look at that way or the one they see as a brother. Only one girl is willing to bypass the sibling sense of relationship, so I seize the opportunity. The intimacy is just a conduit to what I need.

I feed on hearing the words, "I love you."

"I need you."

"You're the best."

"I'm yours forever."

My ears are directly connected to my bloodstream and this audible drug stabilizes both my self esteem and psyche simultaneously. It is satisfying to hear it from the one who took my virginity. They somehow feel true. But her two claims of pregnancy frighten me enough to cause me to leave. When her uterus is due to expand and render physical evidence of it pressing against her belly, she confesses to having abortions—one backyard and the other clinical. I don't believe it. Next time, she will keep it to always have a part of me, she assures me. Negative. I disappear to avoid eighteen years of entrapment at such a young age, but need something new to feed on. So, I find it.

Then, many more find me—too many. Managing my black book of numbers becomes too tedious of a task for me to focus on anything outside of it: school, work, or fun. I spend a lot of time expressing false emotions and denying the other girls that I sometimes put before the one I'm with at the moment. Recognizing the downward spiral, I build up the nerve to deny one, but ten more wait on the other side of the revolving door. Frequent withdrawals require some sort of deposit to balance the chemicals that control my thought process. To satisfy the ailment, I rest my head on the cool side of pink pillowcases, sometimes with the devil himself. No, the women are not the devil, but they are his most powerful device that contribute to my many falls—the others being money, the street mentality, and a crippling affliction.

The first step to recovery is admittance.

Hello. My name is Lil Rob. I have a problem that I cannot overcome on my own. I am addicted to the luscious words women feed me. I can't function without them. My only means to sustain a steady state in my blood is through sex with them. That's the only condition on which they are willing to offer it. I also have an affliction that keeps me from becoming emotionally attached to any female. I compromise my self-respect and dignity for this. I need help.

The second step is identifying its root.

When women swaddle me with their lines, I know they are not genuine. I don't want them to be. If their words represent true emotion, things can grow dangerous. It's the artificial confessions that serve as a hit to sustain me until my next urge arises. As long as I keep a base of women established, I am confident enough to make it through the night—even if it means overlooking all of the risks I take. They are important to me—the words, that is.

"What's the worst that can happen?" is my rationale when considering the facts: I wasn't fond of love growing up and I don't love myself. I never experienced the love of a mother, which is the love most hold dearest to them. The difference in affection and tolerance Ma showed for her kids in contrast to me convinced me that she didn't have it for me either. For instance, she pushed them to finish school if they did nothing else with themselves. She stayed on top of their grades. The last time anyone requested to see a report card of mine was fifth grade. I longed for the sheltering arms others find in siblings but that was absent as well. We were all scattered abroad. I did have Danny from the time he stopped hating me until his death, but that is it. Those who did love me left me to be with God in Heaven at very crucial stages in my life. Thus, to me, no one loves me—especially not these women, not anyone; not even God. Most females fear me and I want to keep it that way. Little do they know, they validate me as someone worthy of living.

This addiction grows greater than an emotional dependency when puberty reaches its peak. Now, it's physical too. The frequent release of testosterone through my encounters causes my body to produce more, resulting in an unhealthy amount of urges. It creates new spasms and my participation in this activity doubles. Thus, the number of women doubles. If it strikes in class, I leave school to satisfy it. Church, I am ditching that too. Two o'clock in the morning can land me in the back seat of a car or in someone's pitch black basement.

It's the curse, I ponder to myself. It's using me as a pawn to take myself out. It must be its new avenue of destruction since I am no longer involved in the street corner aspect of drug dealing.

It is gunning for the monster. Drugs led to him being the victim of violent crime. That brewed anger and caused him to retaliate by participating in those same types of violent crime. None of this brought about love or happiness. The search for the two stewed the private experimentation of narcotics. All of these things attract the women, to complete the equation. Mixed with his ruthlessness, it all adds up to death, in the streets and the bed. Change is inevitable if life is desired. God's call is still waiting. So, to spare my own life, I pursue the life of a preacher.

Yielding to the minister doesn't cause the addiction to vanish. My mannerisms and frame of mind reform when undergoing the ministerial process, but this desire remains the same. The pulpit is the only place I'm not engaging in the act, but I do ponder the thought while there. The authoritative role welcomes a new crowd of even more women to entertain.

I eventually grow uncomfortable—so much so that I seek out a pastor whom I trust to offer guidance and direction. This is a first. If God never knew the true intent of my heart, he should today. I've never sought help in the past for anything—let alone from a man. But it is out of despair. Since I cannot get in touch with God, I will summon his representative.

"You're a man first. As long as you don't pick flowers from your own garden, you will be fine," he advises.

I sit nodding my head in agreement, despite the fact that I am truly confused. I finally realize his only spiritual guidance is for me to refrain from having sex with the girls from the congregation of the church I serve. As ridiculous and "worldly" as it sounds, I still abide in it temporarily to avoid exposure. My targeted audience becomes the women who don't appear in any worship center to expose me on Sunday mornings. But in spite of the real me, God still uses who he called to affect the lives of husbands, sons, grandmothers, pretty single women, children—just to name a few. He illuminates some of the most common and clichéd topics ever preached to open the eyes of the people to a new light, through me. His words pumping through my diaphragm give His children the strength to grasp on to a new sign of hope. I am led to organize an on-campus Bible study group at The University of Maryland-College Park, a few youth programs at different churches, and start evangelizing out on the streets I once ran. It is a humbling experience, but not humbling enough.

With the women I fondle in other places, on Sunday mornings I am considered blameless before man in the church—a corrupt preacher's dream. Stemming from the evident elevation in ministry, I am offered the opportunity to serve as an assistant pastor to different churches and other pastors beckon for me to serve as a youth ministry leader to their congregation. But the more I rock the church, the more I rock the bed, so I decline all offers. They have not taken the time to examine this tree and the fruit that it really bears. Essentially, what they request is for their people to be turned off by my hypocrisy—similar to the way the pastor I confided in turned me off once I saw his true colors. He had no substance. Neither do I at this point.

"God, please forgive me for my sins and please keep from exposing me as I work on true repentance," I pray.

He protects me only for so long. As ministry and my credibility gradually deteriorates, I still continue my search for loving words. Church officials try counseling me because of the many women who appear in the pews to hear me speak. Their words cannot help me. It is too late. I am in too deep. To the left are the women who are members of the church and to the right are ones who are not. The purpose their words serve are the only ones I am interested in.

"Aren't you supposed to be a preacher?"

There aren't more convicting words from others after witnessing the vulgar phrases that proceed from my mouth, the many different girls I parade through the church, and the funds accumulated from drug dealing. The best answer I muster up is not that I am sorry or that I repent, but that, "I'm a man first!"

I am right. That's what I am taught. That's what I prove

myself to be, just a man—not the good man I want to be, not even a real man. As a preacher, I don't commit myself fully to God. Being blessed enough to avoid exposure in the church, led to being exposed to the risk of contracting sexually transmitted diseases and the malicious intent of women instead. I jeopardize my health practicing unsafe sex and being made known later on that I was once exposed to herpes, the human papillomavirus (or HPV), trichomoniasis and gonorrhea—the ones women told me of after the fact. They claimed to have found out when they told me and had no prior knowledge of it.

"You should get yourself checked because I found out I have…" is the rehearsed lines spoken each time.

Luckily, I dodged most of these bullets. But in due season, I contract one. I can only assume who it comes from because only one of the women I am currently involved with shares this infection. She mentions the possibility that it could've been me to carry it for some time and give it to her. Sadly, I can't argue that. I've never been tested prior to this.

The most embarrassing thing to appear at the registration desk of the emergency room for is to be treated for an STD. I wait for hours to be seen.

The doctor walks in.

"Ok, sir. What seems to be the problem?"

"I need to be treated for an STD."

"Which one?"

"All of them."

"You have every STD?"

"No. I don't know. I just need to be treated."

"How about we test you for an STD first, because we cannot just treat you and give you a prescription for antibiotics without first finding out what it is we are treating?"

"Cool."

I stand to put this robe on as directed by the doctor, but I don't understand why. I expect him to come in with just a cup for me to give a sample of urine. He has to take blood too, but that still does not explain the robe. I see him pull a Q-tip about eight inches in length from the cabinet.

"What are you going to do with that?"

"Mr. Douglas, I have to insert this into your penis to see if you are having any discharge. This is the test for gonorrhea. It's not as bad as it looks. You hold it and I will insert it."

He is right, it is not a bad as it looks. It's worse. He twists it once he gets it as far as he can and pulls it out, places it into a container, calls a nurse to take my blood and asks me to pee in a cup.

Hours later, he walks in and says, "You have trich [thrichomoniasis]."

I respond by making a puzzling face. The doctor fights to bridle his laughter but is unsuccessful. Thanks be to God, a disabling shot of penicillin to the rear end and two weeks of antibiotics kill the parasite, but unfortunately, does not kill my desires.

I reform for about two weeks before the withdrawals grow greater and the phone rings longer too. Soon, I am back out feasting without protection.

This addiction brings on a loss of integrity, strength, and dignity. This demon's grasp takes hold of me as he sinks his venomous nails into my back and we roll around with one another underneath the sheets. It flourishes through the phases of depression. So to cope, I conveniently deliver myself into the devil's playground—only to stress over other false pregnancy claims and frequent phone calls to trace the origins of other sexually transmitted diseases. Thankfully, I wasn't the one to carry, transport, or contract anymore of them after the first.

Afflictions

"Affliction comes to us, not to make us sad but sober—not to make us sorry but wise."
–Henry Ward Beecher

THOUGH MANY ADDICTIONS FORMING FROM mere curiosities penetrate the veins of this broken vessel, the afflictions operate independently. They stem from a mental condition that no medication can cure. Being knowledgeable of its growth but unaware of its origin becomes very problematic. I can't stop it. Some speak of the issue with little concern, but this stronghold causes self-inflicted suffering, leaving me without work, a home, and unable to finish college. It jams the chamber to the gun used for my one shot at success, leaving me desperate for another hopeless attempt.

This thing, this monstrosity is often called commitment anxiety.

I challenge those who dare say they suffer from this disorder, but only in regard to aspects of their lives such as intimate relationships. If that be the case, the agony and inferiority I endure daily will remain unfathomable because it affects every portion of my life. Its controlling dominance forces me to act against my own will. The level of greed and ravenousness in it rages too wildly to settle for one area of my everyday life—it's a principality that no one knows how to overcome. Most afflictions work from the external, thus it can be easily isolated. But this is an internal demon. Because of it, my life is in shambles today.

I toil to get there. Ma evicts me and I still fulfill the requirements of my senior year in spite of the unknown—where I will lay my head when wrestling practice ends—but then I blow it. From sleeping in cars, taking showers in the locker room and enduring the mental strain of being accepted into college, I let it slip away. Even with the money, time, space, and energy people sacrificed to provide me necessities, I still make excuses. When that well runs dry, I make another. The spew I spit to myself and others, having to work full-time to maintain stability outside of school, is true, but it is also the only excuse that masks my disability. Next to the intimidation of my surroundings—where every other college student's needs are met by others in order to fully focus on their twenty-page research papers—I am afraid of committing to success. The probability of failure runs too great. I grew so fond of failing in the past because I surrounded myself with dead-end opportunities for so long—or should I say it surrounded me.

My ambition to receive a high school diploma is not just to be the first in my family's generation and the first in the streets I run to achieve this, but to prove the nay-sayers wrong. College is a bit more challenging academically, although my transcripts suggest that there is a drastic increase in the level of difficulty. Nonetheless, I take it on to do the same as before. Yet, when something as outlandish as this golden opportunity presents itself, the anxiety causes me to shut it down. The reaction is involuntary. I am just too weak to resist.

No matter the opportunity, this condition sedates me to be easily convinced to pass it on—so I retract myself from it to await a more worthwhile opportunity. I am waiting, still. I now realize those were the cards dealt to me and because I thought I was worthy of a better hand to increase my probability of winning, I threw it in. I had two aces: an acceptance into the University of Maryland-College Park and a full-scholarship to attend, and a couple of spades: money saved up and familiar faces on a campus with 36,000 students. But to me, I will still lose without the big and little jokers: mom and dad to rear me—which everyone else seems to have.

I still have my Heavenly Father, right? Can He help me to see this journey to the end? I go to His house to find out. Initially, my appearance at this place is due to my desire to impress a young lady's father. What better way to stroke the ego of a pastor than to show up at church and pretend his words affect your life in some way. That day though, he didn't preach. An outof-town visitor from Texas did.

The visiting minister begins laying hands on people and slaying them in the spirit. My exact words to one of the preacher's daughters are, "Is this real?"

Her head springs into my direction in astonishment at my audacity to question religious practices, but as that emotion settles, I see she doesn't know herself. "I don't know, honestly. Find out," she confesses, big-eyed and smirking.

There is no better man for the job. If I prove him to be a false prophet, I can give up on the idea of Him altogether and the issue will be resolved. I met this pastor the night prior to this service. He seemed nice. So I hate what I prepare to do to him. Then again, after all of the dung God drags me through year after year, I must channel my anger through someone. Today, it will be him.

I stand to my feet to view all of the bodies lying prostrate at the altar. The women have blankets draped over their legs to cover the openings of their dresses. But the attention is taken off the corpses once I rise. The people are quiet. I slide past everyone in the row and enter the aisle. I can turn and head toward the bathroom, but approach the altar to take my position in line instead. As the people before me continue to fall like dominoes, I am now at the front of the line. The preacher stands before me. Another clergy member anoints his hands with oil. His cold palms graze the center of my forehead as he speaks.

"Yesterday when we met, I gained a great deal of respect for you. I don't take to people easily, but there's something powerful inside of you; greater than me and anyone I have ever met. Tap into it and use it for good, son. Now as we pray, if you feel the spirit move you, don't fight it. But if you don't, just pray."

He reads my thoughts. The oil must give him this power. He knows I seek to reveal the truth and even if I am wrong, I will fight the feeling and never tell. I nod anyway. We bow our heads and close our eyes and about four hands land on my shoulders simultaneously. My hands are also intertwined with the fingers of soft, wrinkly hands now. I try to listen to the prayers being extended toward Heaven on my behalf, but am distracted by the random outbursts of praise from the older members of the church. As we pray, my body stiffens gradually. My knees buckle, arms straighten, and I am squeezing the fragile hands that crumble in my palms involuntarily. It can't be! I fling my eyes open to focus on something else. I try to regain the activity of my limbs when my entire body starts convulsing—violently. I blurt incomprehensible sounds and collapse, still paralyzed. The sight seen is indescribable, but there is a light too bright to focus on and open hands.

All I hear in the calmest tone is, "Call on me."

The shouting of others in the church is drowned out by this voice. Sprawled on the floor, soaking the carpet with both sweat and tears, I scream, "Jesus," repeatedly. That's all I can think to say.

Nearly a half hour later, God is done with my wimpy cries and relinquishes to me control over my muscular system. Church is over. Everyone is gone. I just lie there. The vibrations of music and laughter seep through the floorboards. The once paralyzed congregation is now gathered downstairs. I try to be embarrassed, but don't have enough strength to be. What just happened, is all I wonder. I'm still unsure whether being slain in the spirit is a real state. I don't want to find out. But my spirit of rebellion and anger still exists. Maybe God just wanted to teach me to respect Him, which I lacked until now. I also learn to never put the Lord God to the test. Never will I again. If I never really believed in Jesus or the presence of God before, I do now.

I crack my Bible open reading fifteen chapters a night after that experience, needing answers. Over time, all I find is a calling for my life and sudden desire to lead people in a way that will change the game, which is what I inevitably did in the drug world. It was always in me—so much so that I used it for evil. That's what that preacher meant by, "using it for good," I assume. With this new revelation, I commit to it but awaken to hell on earth when I receive a bill from school.

I am envious of my college roommate, Marcus. He is a magician. If a need arises, he simply picks up the phone and magically a package appears at the front desk addressed to him within two days. His greatest trick is to make that Ford Expedition with the Marine Corp stickers on the rear window appear within a few hours if the need is dire. I couldn't quite master the alakazam. If I don't meet my own need, it leaves a void and impacts my grades along with my temperament. When I go without my greatest need, however, disaster strikes.

I continue my endeavors for a solution. I have no home away

from my dorm room and no family apart from my roommate. He does his best to ease my pain by stuffing his belly button with cotton and crackers to drive me crazy. His big gut made the exact same face as Danny's, same complexion and all. However, Marcus goes home when school is out and I need shelter during seasonal breaks. Apparently, the department of resident life is naïve enough to believe that everyone has somewhere to stay, so they close the dorms. None of my real friends have places of their own. My only option is to irk the nerves of their residential directors until they permit me to stay. They charge me to sleep in a lounge during Thanksgiving and spring breaks and in an on-campus apartment for winter and summer breaks. Those charges accumulate, but my scholarship program doesn't cover housing outside of normal semester months. Neither does financial aid. So I am left with the tab.

Waltzing up to the Lee Building to meet with my financial advisor and accept the loan offered to me in my aid packet shouldn't be a struggle.

"What? How am I denied a loan you already offered to give me? That makes no sense!" my voice rises.

Now, I need a co-signer. I don't even know anyone willing to house me. When I first enrolled in school, receiving financial aid was a hassle because Ma was still my legal guardian but she refused to submit her tax information to the school. Even though I was offered a full scholarship, they claimed to only be allowed to pay a small amount for each student and the rest was to be covered by the government. With Ma's refusal, I had no choice but to file as an independent student. At my age, the one criterion that allowed me to do so is if both of my parents were deceased. This sparked the journey to find my father.

I obtain a list of phone numbers registered under the same name as my father, in the same place I was born, and around the age he should be and beg my roommate to call each of them. I just couldn't. He did, but it rendered no results. Without my father's death certificate or information, I am not eligible for financial assistance. Sitting in the office draining my tear ducts from crying convinces the director to bypass the requirements and buy me time to either locate my father or soften up Ma enough to get what I need. The odds favor me finding my father. But I don't. In the eyes of the government, without the documentation, there is no proof that my father does not support me financially and cannot contribute to my education. I do not make enough legal tender to prove I support myself, hence the reason I now need a co-signer. They couldn't be more wrong.

With such an outstanding bill, I cannot register for classes. I have to withdraw.

Before I do, I want to discuss this with someone. Somebody can help. There are plenty who are available, but the anxiety persuades me to head straight to the registrar's office to sign the papers of intent not to return before it is too late. It is the last day to do so. A sense of urgency governs my gait. I reluctantly comply. The form asks for a reason.

Well, I write, the university doesn't have the major of my interest. I am leaving to attend Bible College.

It isn't a lie because a feeling that God led me to that office comes over me. It's now my duty to step out on faith and trust Him. With a detailed plan to execute what I stepped out on faith for, I have yet to see a day of Bible College. Unbeknownst to me, I cannot owe one institution and attend another on financial assistance. I lied after all, but putting it on God somehow made it feel true.

Without college as a crutch, I am now officially rendered homeless. If only they let me into that big mansion with Danny.

I reach out to the church but receive no physical support: just prayer. The same pastor to offer his advice before tells me, "You don't need your own place right now. You're screwing enough women as it is," and laughs out loud. I miss the joke.

I beg Ma to shelter me in my storm. She agrees, but it isn't long before I'm back out on the streets without any justification as to why. Overnight, rumors of me verbally abusing her and taking advantage of her vulnerable state are spread and my entire family despises me, again. When she accepts me, they accept me. But when she loathes the thought of my name, so do they. With nowhere to turn, I make my bed and lay in it in the back seat of my 1994 Mazda MPV. Every piece of clothing I own keeps me warm. Finally, when I grow as comfortable as possible, the van is too stripped from me. It breaks down after leaving me with many fines and tickets to pay for driving uninsured. These add to the list of bills to be paid before I can proceed with life.

I lose everything. I have nothing. When I have nothing, I find everything—God and the promises of the Bible. I dive in to find answers because I am petrified of sleeping outside now. I get goose bumps rubbing against strangers in public, let alone the possibility of them sitting on me as I sleep on the bus stop bench. Homeless addicts plague the china house, so I cannot go back there. They attract police. All of the grief I dealt could possibly cause someone to wreak havoc on me. Without answers, I realize this is my night to die.

As I search for a safe and dry place to rest, I am spared in the nick of time. Someone answers my plea and invites me in. The roaches here are the least of my worries. Every new day brings a new last minute cot or futon until one gracious family houses me for about a year. The next two years, I bounce between sheltering locations. Humiliated and uncomfortable, being totally dependent on another man to care for this fully competent one, I do appreciate their help. The discomfort motivates me to recover, but I am too depressed to make a change.

Every door I pry open, God deliberately shuts and double locks. Even the streets no longer accept me. My inconsistency keeps the most desperate hustlers from fronting me another pack. The only way in is for me to purchase my own product to sell and find a territory to establish as my own. Every corner is occupied. The negativity everyone once claimed for my life is coming to pass. Those are the only words that sink in because I can see the manifestation of them in my life. For years I was told I wouldn't amount to anything. Now, look at me. I am nothing.

A positive voice came along once, expecting to uproot the years of negativity sown into my heart. It was my best friend, Ashley Parker. I met her my first year of college. She was still in high school then but was visiting the university, a prospect school of hers. I like to think my presence sealed the deal for her to attend. A mutual friend of ours was her tour guide and brought Ashley and another friend of hers to my room. I heard the knock and slid out the door to stand in the hallway with them. My room was a mess from the night before, so I was embarrassed to let them in. I am introduced to the two and jokingly say to Ashley, "Let me see your feet," to break the ice.

Facebook and instant messaging kept us in connection with one another until she started her first day at Maryland. A year later, she is the reason for my housing arrangements, after beckoning her family members to come to my rescue.

She walks into the office of her parent's house one day, where I stay. She's coming from school.

"I'm worthless, Ashley."

"Stop saying that! You are a good person, Robert. There aren't many out here like you. Why can't you see that?"

"Look at me! Take a good look at me, at my life! What do I have to offer? Huh? I can't hear you. Nothing! I live off you and your parents! I ain't, never was, and never will be anything! I serve God day in and day out and this is what I get in return? All I do is help people, but can't even help my self! That's what I see."

"You have everything to offer, Robert. You may not see it now, but I do. I don't see you for who you are now. I see you for who you will become and where you are going in life. You are an amazing man. Look at all of the lives you've impacted and the people you help. Who else do you see having this affect on others at your age? People need you and look up to you, even people who you may not think. You would be selfish to give up now. Just have faith. It's coming. This is just temporary."

"Whatever. Let me see you go through it."

She sighs.

Though it's not accepted, I need that. Still, her words fall on deaf ears because she is alone in offering this positive reinforcement. The problem is the people I need to hear it from are absent in my life. My pastor, family, and friends left their roles vacant and she is the one desiring to fill every position. She doesn't realize the impossible nature of the task. The women I'm involved with don't care to see my inner core. Their tunnel vision can only see the glorious light that falls on me through preaching. They want to partake in it but I never keep them around long enough to. I despise Ashley even though she is my best friend. I push her away because I want to prove to her that she too will soon abandon me—just like God and the rest of the world. They all receive what they please and I never hear from them again. So, I keep my distance. When I sold drugs, I had it all but when I came to God, I lost it all. Now operating in my spiritual gift, I only hear His voice to receive direction for other individuals. As for my personal life, He grows mute.

Through it all though, Ashley's feet are shod in her beliefs of me whether I accept them or not. Her greatest quality is that I don't have to solicit her words via sexual encounters, but she offers them voluntarily. This one woman schools me on what is second nature to most: that love is a choice and I must choose to love myself before I find contentment. She thinks I hate myself. I do. I hate my father too, but it's my fault he left—so I hate myself for that. Everything in my life is my fault. Mom dying is my fault. Danny being killed is my fault. Neighborhood kids growing to be the same ruthless individual as myself is my fault. I hooked their mothers and fathers to crack and dope. It's me, but outwardly, I pass the blame onto others. Internally is where the real battle lies.

Realizing this doesn't help me leave the women alone—not just yet. I still need them. I have no intentions of loving them. They just help me feel better about myself. These chains that hold me prisoner won't be released. If I commit, I am free, ironically. It can't happen, as hard as I try. I don't want any woman to commit to me anyway. Not in this condition.

I finally find a job, but the affliction strikes too fast for me to put a stop to it. In a hopeless state both academically and financially, I weigh my options. I studied criminology in school to go on to work for the Drug Enforcement Agency. Marcus and I agreed that our starting grounds would be the local police department after graduation. I don't need a degree to be a cop, so I apply. Thus, I will accomplish the goals I set out to achieve, after a few detours. I am not a police officer. They did call me with a conditional offer of employment. When the opportunity does knock, I freeze. I just know there is something else for me and I don't want to settle into a career that will confine my availability.

This is all for some greater being's entertainment. I am sure of it. Sometimes I have to view my life from external eyes to see the truth. Many believe I embellish. They see this smile and refuse to believe in the pain that hides behind it. I look at the faces others try to fight off when they look at my life and I wish it was embellished. Sadly, it isn't, and to see other's external perspective of me, I can only imagine their thoughts:

"It's just a shame. He lacks common sense. He has so much potential that goes unused because of the entrapment of his mind. If I were a homeless, drug-dealing kid that made it into a prestigious school free of charge and was awarded the opportunity to be the first in my entire family to earn a bachelor's degree, I would kill myself if I screwed that up. Really, he's done just that. He was provided complimentary food and shelter in addition to a free education, yet he convinces himself within his own feeble little mind that there is something better offered to a young, inner city male with no credentials. No opportunities are given in this day. From the words of Sir Frances Bacon, 'A wise man will make more opportunities than he finds.' How can he make an opportunity without first capitalizing on the ones that he does find? There are people who aren't nearly as intelligent as he, but work their bottoms off to get to the top."

"He left school to attend Washington Bible College, which isn't a bad move. The fact that he has yet to attend doesn't convince me that God authorized it because where God gives a vision, he too gives the knowledge and understanding of when to move, along with the provision to fund it. From newspaper articles to the cover of a university magazine, he has all eyes on him just to later fill them with tears."

"Even though God spares him from having to sleep on the street, he still has no stable residence two years after the very day he left school. He desires employment but can't overcome the twoyear commitment that is required by the police department for all new employees. His only account of success is to one day be a good father and husband. He can't even achieve this with his current state of mind. One day he will stand at the altar with his bride and say, 'I don't,' because there are many women for him to consider before that decision is made. Or maybe someone will one day mother his child and will be forced to file for child support because he decides that there is a woman out there who can produce a better kid by him so he leaves them to find that woman."

"His claim to commitment anxiety doesn't stop him from committing six years of his life to the dangers of the streets. Oh, of course, at the time there were no greater opportunities because it surrounded him by every which-a-way. Granted he had no one to pave the way, an abundance of resources were provided for him. He had no computer; one of his high school teachers bought him one. His laptop was stolen and the university gave him one. He needed money for books, the school awarded him a refund check that was ample the amount needed. Of course he had other needs but instead of continuing to work, he resorted to drug dealing there as well. That is the more worthwhile opportunity he abandons everything else for. That will be all he ever amounts to until he allows himself to be set free. I understand he had no financial backing, which left him working overnight at UPS and struggling to attend classes during the day, but to be that persistent just to give in bewilders me. All of those who have empathized with him have been let down by him time and time again. So I don't."

I am on the prowl for what I searched for my entire life. I strike success, finally, when I locate my father. He's not my biological father but will do. He satisfies every requirement of my checklist— to be stern, wealthy, and proud, which is all I know a real man to be. The misconstrued perception in the fatherless streets I grew up in can attest to that. These are also the common qualities of the few in the hood that dare father their children. So, I find the most puffed-up, proud individual on the face of the earth to adopt me. He promises respect, monetary compensation, honor, the perks of being his own, and what is most important to me, the courage to be a good man. I buy into his seducing words of milk and honey because we enter into contract and I commit to developing into the polar opposite of my real father. Americans often refer to him as an uncle, but I call him daddy—Daddy Sam. I enlisted in the United States Army as an active duty soldier, under a four-year contract to show that commitment is no longer my issue. I refuse to be taunted by internal thoughts that persuade me that homelessness and depression are all I deserve.

As a Signals Intelligence Analyst, I am scheduled to appear in Missouri for my basic combat training. Following, I will be stationed in Texas for eleven months for my advanced individual training. Only God knows my destination thereafter—and thereafter the thereafter. I didn't seek Him in this process because His voice is now strange to me. Even if I could miraculously distinguish His words again, I know it will be for me to stew in the fecal matter of the same nay-sayers that predicted this storm in my life, which they declared, will devour me. So, I make the rash decision to prove them wrong. I need a job along with shelter and food. More importantly, I need to make my own way.

I didn't enlist as a chaplain because only the officers get the opportunity to speak. My zeal would be bridled. I'm fine with that. I need time. The wrongdoing witnessed and heard of in the church ignites my youthful ignorance and sends me seeking to expose the corrupt ones for the sake of the people. In the army, it would be foolish to expose an officer, so this is for the best. Besides, I am not stable enough in ministry. I turn it on and off like a light switch. When I suffer troubles and it becomes too difficult for me, I turn it off and vice versa. So I am just as guilty as the others. After seeing the wrongful deeds of some and the complacency of others in leadership, I bounce from church-to-church with every step like my ground is a trampoline. If I spent more time exposing myself, I wouldn't be faced with some of the calamity in my life today.

So I choose Signals Intelligence. This commitment I cannot retract myself from. Time to pack.

Every one that is proud in heart is an abomination to the LORD: though hand join in hand, he shall not be unpunished.
-Proverbs 16:5

These words haunt me daily. In some form, I hear it on the radio and on the TV, and read it on billboards and in my Bible. Today, I decide my pride has damaged my soul enough. It creates a spirit of avoidance when it is peace from conflict and confrontation that I seek. As I expected, it only welcomes more chastisement. My current location should be Good Fellows Air Force Base, but I sit in the chapel of Northwest Hospital—Baltimore, Maryland—where I work in dietary. I wasn't tough enough to graduate from basic training. No, the exercise wasn't unbearable. The yelling from drill instructors didn't get to me. I didn't purposefully injure myself or pretend to have gone "loco" in order to earn an honorable discharge. I didn't graduate basic training because I never left for it.

Again, another inconsistency, another opportunity deferred to return to a state of nothingness. Some thought this affliction to be a figment of my imagination but it is alive and well.

Here I am at the Military Enlistment Processing Station scheduled to ship out when the first sergeant desperately tries to sound intimidating, "Army shipper Douglas! Stand in this line!"

It is actually the wrong line for me to be in. These folk are headed to Fort Benning. I point out the mishap to the now humiliated army man. Once that situation is rectified, they prepare my airplane tickets and cashier's check for food.

Now in the correct line and on the way to the bus, "I'm not going," I mumble to the first sergeant.

As hard as I fight what begins to embody me, it is the victor. My exhaustive efforts prior to this date to locate medical records and court documents, to pay off debts, and even to have surgery at my expense before shipping out, prove to be in vain. I referred others to enlist, trained daily, memorized the soldier's creed and met every other requirement of Dad's, but my feet did not leave the ground.

I must remain hidden from public scrutiny. How can the minister return to church after the going-away dinner where everyone begged him to stay? The ones who did approve said it would be to my benefit because I would finally learn some discipline. I must be comfortable with returning to a state of nothingness subconsciously, when the Army offered to meet my every need and I refused my ticket to abandon this dry and desolate land. I grew afraid of such a great commitment and backed out—as always.

I cannot be seen. My pride won't allow it. But I couldn't locate my pride as I prepared to board that bus to head to the airport, or when I needed it to protect me from the disappointing stares I got when I came home in plain clothing. It stood boldly as I convinced everyone the right decision for me was to go. Surely it didn't falter when I signed the contract and swore in as an official United States soldier.

How can I ever be an inspiration to others if I cannot inspire myself to aspire for more? Back to the drawing board it is for me.

Submissions

Submit yourselves therefore to God. Resist the devil, and he will flee from you.
-James 4:7

AS I HEAR THE TAIL end of this phrase, resist the devil and he will flee from you, I wonder. The more I resist, the more he seeks to prove that he is more powerful. With his success, he proves to be accurate. Resistance is not the key, but is all I know. I learned resistance in the streets and even as I try to resist the streets, they constantly call my name. The demons, the women, and the destruction that haunt me day in and day out camoflauge themselves to overcome my resistance and conquer me. The act of resisting the devil alone will not make him flee. It will make him return with other demons seven times stronger. Submission unto God is key— which is surely not my particular area of expertise thus my demons penetrate me as they so desire.

I submit to my own authority. That's what the streets taught me. Society even teaches these same laws. Women are never urged to submit to a man, but to stand as an individual who is equal to all (as if submission decreases your value as a human). The black boys from my neck of the woods are raised to never submit to the white man's tyranny. Children even these days are told to pave a way for themselves to find their true identities as opposed to submitting to the desires of their parents. That is the rap submission gets where I am from. To submit means to be weak, so not even the three piece suits I hide behind in the pulpit can bring me to true submission. It's taboo. To survive in this type of environment requires much self-centeredness. But for me, the time has come—in more ways than one.

Submit: (verb) (1.) to propose or to hand in; to give up, (2.) to commit to something in consideration of another, (3.) to yield or accept one's authority.

(1.) to propose or to hand in; to give up

I must admit, there is a remnant of control that my demons still possess. I am blindly submitted to them. Their treachery lies in forcing me to believe I am in control. But I cannot stop it. Pimping me on the street corners, which made me ruthless, was not what I wanted; I wanted to focus on school. Stripping me of my family through death and resentment, stripping me of opportunities, and of all dignity and pride left me hopeless when I didn't want that to be my reaction. I was persuaded that the feelings I experienced were natural. Sadness, yes—depression, maybe; but feelings of self-destruction, suicide, and loss of all self-esteem were not. An offering of verbal therapy was the only thing worth holding on to. It makes living to see another day worthwhile. Until one day, my demons grow desperate and send a one night stand my way.

I am careful not to hook up with people who are new associates. This method is my mainstream defense against any disease and a way of being health conscious, as if my past experiences don't exist. This time is different. Every time is. But it is this time because this woman is different. She is a former classmate, so we are acquaintances. I haven't seen her since first grade but we still recognize one another, so that counts for something. Reminiscing on things we both vaguely remember, she recalls a letter she wrote to me. She can't remember my last name but can remember walking down to Hollywood, a playground where I hung out with her brother and other friends, to give it to me. We called it Hollywood because that was our paradise. It had three sets of swings, two sliding boards, monkey bars, a jungle gym, see-saws, and basketball and tennis courts to name a few things. Everything was in working order too. There was no other playground like it in our area. It was our only escape from the projects.

The letter apparently requested that I check the box corresponding to whether or not I was interested in her. Allegedly, I tore it up. I can believe it. First grade was a tough year for me. I floated in and out of schools each year which made it difficult to make friends. I attended five elementary schools: Tench Tilman, William Paca, General Wolfe, Commodore John Rogers, and Highlandtown Elementary—a new school for each grade seemingly. Only a few classmates remember my transient presence today. Those are the ones who lived in Chapel Hill Projects (C.H.P.) with us. Everyone who was tough enough to survive the torture of Chapel Hill's A.T.H. crew (athletes, thugs and hustlers) vowed C.H.P. for life. We couldn't forget one another. This young lady is affiliated with that community.

Somehow this trip down memory lane has a sofa bed at the end of it, where we lay entangled with one another that same night.

Approximately three minutes into this reunion, she screams, "Oh my God, I love you!"

Her eyes are full of mockery, pupils dilated. This demon, through her, stares at this pathetic individual, both amused and empowered. But this is nothing out of the ordinary to hear. In fact, it is normally my intention when involving myself with women. I sought to hear them, so why are her words so bothersome?

She knows nothing about me. If she knew of my past and even my present practices, she too would turn her back on me. I wish she had enough self-respect not to allow me to have unprotected sex with her. If only she knew how many people I have been with unprotected—and the STD I contracted. I should warn her that I cut off every woman the second she complains of a missed period or nausea. Then, I'm off to find others. But, she should know this already if she loves me. She should know that I'm stupid enough to pride myself on the pulling out method I mastered to prevent unwanted pregnancies. That's me. And no woman in her right mind could love such a creature. I don't love such a creature. I'm tired of the false love even if it's all I know.

I am a fool to believe things are in my power. Like a car though, you don't realize how much you have spun out of control until it takes you in a direction you do not wish to go. Something has to stop me before I crash and burn, or worse.

"What?" I say, hoping to hear, "Nothing," as a response in order for this charade to continue.

Instead, "I said I love you baby," she moans, eyes filled with blood.

My motion halts, "You love me? Yo, you don't even know me!" Up, already halfway dressed, "You gotta go." She sighs.

"Now!" I scream.

I gain momentum. She tries to convince me that her words are simply in the moment. My mind is preoccupied by the torment of flashbacks of women who used me, afflicted me, and manipulated their ways back into my life once they were cut off. But I allowed it. As a high school kid, a hustler, college student, and minister, I allowed them. No longer will I.

I give up. I hand in this lifestyle and submit my claim to this addiction. I turn away from my promiscuity once and for all. It once bore the burden for a lack of love, but now holds no merit. The undying bliss is greater when there is meaning behind them— even more special when compensation is not required.

The one thing to ward me off this addicting substance is to submit to the true love of God, to know that even as I lay in bed with devils and demons, He loves me. Even after I abandoned Him, He still loves me. When I didn't love myself, He loved me. The thoughts of suicide and other hedonistic acts didn't stop Him from loving me. He was there loving me the same then as He does now. So I don't depend on the love of women or those family members who forsook me any longer. He loves me, and there is nothing that can separate me from His love.

For I am persuaded, that neither death, nor life, nor angels, nor principalities, nor powers, nor things present, nor things to come, nor height, nor depth, nor any other creature, shall be able to separate us from the love of God, which is in Christ Jesus our Lord.
-Romans 8:38-39

(2.) to commit to something in consideration of another

I sit myself down from preaching before anyone else is hypocritical enough to do so. I'm not living right and it's starting to show. Now, five months later, I am expecting a child and am not married. The fact that I am unwilling to undergo a crash wedding before my child's mother shows evidence of pregnancy ticks off those same pastors who have children, but not from any of their multiple marriages. Though I wish I was married before children came into play, for financial stability and because of my religious beliefs, God makes no mistakes and my daughter is no mistake. She is well worth giving up my privilege to step into the pulpit.

The mother of my child, my best friend and now emotional partner is Ms. Ashley Parker. Ashley is the only one to truly love me, the one to help me love myself. She continually focuses on my positive attributes as I, along with the world, view the negative. She is there to suffer with me through the valley and to celebrate on the mountain tops. But this self-love is not the same as the love I expressed for myself in the streets. This love is patient, like Ashley's love.

As my friend, when I involve myself in other relations filled with lust, she is there to warn me but still support me in my decision to stay. My rampage on women resurfaces and she stands there to correct me but catch my tears after ignoring her advice. Her friendship is a refuge for me to retreat to in time of need. Permanently residing at this haven brings peace and rest. She is nothing but patient with me.

Love is kind. With nowhere to go, she pleads with her family to open their doors, arms, and hearts to a man they barely know. Her passion is convincing enough for them. She struggles to maintain her college GPA and works to help support me financially, keep gas in her car to transport me to different engagements, and anywhere else my heart desires. She is full of kindness.

Love does not envy. I have nothing for her to envy, so that is easy for her.

Love does not boast. Two years after being housed under her parent's roof, riding in her passenger seat, and reaping the fruits of her labor, I get to my knees—not quite to my feet. I have yet to hear it mentioned or regurgitated to gain leverage in any dispute or argument. When I try to repay her, she suddenly suffers from amnesia.

The list goes on. I owe her my heart. Her humility deserves that at the least. The fruits of a union such as this teaches me a new love—the love of a father for my unborn daughter whom we now await.

Unfortunately, with our baby yet to be born, the affliction and anxieties flare up. With two at-home pregnancy tests, an obstetrics visit and a prenatal ultrasound to confirm conception, I flee the scene. Nobody understands. It's not my baby that I want to leave. I don't know what it is. But she can't make me stay.

"I can't deal with Ashley's emotional instability and I don't want her to drive me to the point of no return. All we do is argue constantly. So I had to leave," I gripe and try convincing myself.

She's begging me to stay. I block it out.

And now, after years of desiring to see my real father, I do. He lies in the image of me because of the actions I take.

No! I'm not like him. He dealt with Mom's emotions when she had Quinshawna. He knew what to expect when having me. Plus, I didn't hook my child's mother to drugs, cigarettes, and alcohol, are my thoughts as I stare into this piece of glass at my reflection. So what if my abuse of alcohol has sky-rocketed. It has nothing to do with this.

"But you left her just like he left your mom," I hear in my head.

I drink to escape the picture that rests on the face of the mirror, which doesn't look exactly like me, but somehow shows a strong resemblance. This bottle also helps cope with Ashley's whines as she begs me to stay. One day in particular, too many drinks lead to assaults on folk from my past and in my drunkenness, I see Mom too. This is the first I see the two together. They split me right down the middle at that moment; fifty percent Mr. Robinson and fifty percent Mom. My drunken state aids in expressing my wrath, like Mom.

Like the time Mom comes to my Uncle Ben's barbershop to see me. She is so drunk. Her hair is curled and contrasts the red tent to her face. Her eyes are bloodshot and she has a long brown paper bag in her left hand. She is left-handed, so am I. Uncle Ben doesn't want me to see her this way, so he locks her out of the shop to shelter me. She grows furious as she yells and receives no reply.

"Let me see my son! Man-Man, open the door, baby," she screeches. I rise.

"Bobby, don't you go to that door," my uncle demands. I hate it when he calls me Bobby. I told him before but he just won't stop. Bobby is a name for boys who are juniors and I am not. "Poncella, go home!" he continues.

I take the seat right in front of the window this time to see out of it. Mom throws her brown paper bag at the door and breaks the empty glass inside of it. She takes off running.

Like my father, I avoid and neglect my child's mother. I glance down at my phone: 47 missed calls, eleven text messages, and an email all from her, pleading that I answer. She wants to know if I will take her to tomorrow's prenatal appointment. I try to deny my evident intoxication but the empty bottles of cranberry juice that are mixed with 99 apples aren't so easy to hide. Before I can reply with my answer, no, I pass out right there on the step.

Hung over the next day, I think about my niece when leaving the stoop I fell asleep on. Danny was killed just around the corner from here. What would he think? I stop; think of my baby girl and of Ashley. I would hate for my daughter to grow to be a writer and scribe about how much she despises Robert Arthur Douglas for the burns she suffers from a coward such as me. So, I go to that appointment as a father, not Ashley's partner.

She nags me the entire ride on how worried she was last night. We pull up and walk in. The visit is brief. Towards the end, I hear a repetition of thumps and static through this instrument the doctor is holding. It is the movement of our little girl and her heartbeat. It beats so fast yet causes a serene feeling to fall over me. I fall in love with the sound. Ashley looks at me and smiles. I can't help but do the same. That's our seed. I can't allow my family to be broken so that one day my child will inquire as to why.

"Do you have any questions, Pop?" the doctor asks.

"Um, just one. Is there anything you can prescribe her [Ashley] to stabilize her moods?" is my attempt to seek help and eliminate my excuse. After all, I do love her.

"There's nothing for her. That's a part of pregnancy. There are a lot of new hormones that her body is unfamiliar with. They are in such great levels that they cause her mood to sway. She can't control it. But I do have something for you."

"Ok, good. What?" my curiosity peaks.

"The New Testament," I hear over his shoulder as he walks out.

I just stare at the ground, reflecting on a particular passage of this New Testament that I preached in January of 2007—1 Corinthians 13:4-7. The church was on their feet shouting at the closing remarks of my sermon as pastors fought to recruit me. I felt

117

like a first round pick in the draft. I have no license yet, just a calling. Years later, I realize the minister doesn't institute the principles he urges others to. I am not these things with Ashley. In that tiny office, I break the cycle of my family and decide to love my daughter and Ashley in the proper manner. I commit to my family, first for myself and in consideration of the two.

Ashley and Moriah Nicole Douglas, our daughter—with a name developed from Hebrew, Greek and Gaelic to mean chosen by Jehovah (God) to have victory for the people in dark waters—I love you and I submit myself to you.

(3.) to yield or accept one's authority

On my own agenda, I take authority over my calling, but uphold the façade for people to continue to pat me on the back. I feel wanted, needed. However, I grow weary of being forced to stand before a congregation each week in a wrinkled suit to declare how good and faithful God is when I can't see the manifestation of it in my own life currently. These people have a home to go to after service. I don't. I approach the podium to encourage people to have hope when I no longer possess it myself. Somehow, I pull it off.

"Lift up your heads, O ye gates; even lift them up, ye everlasting doors; and the King of glory shall come in," is what comes out when I want to say, "Where is God in my situation? How is it that He can use me for your benefit, but not my own? I'm finished with this."

I am still homeless.

I am still helpless.

I am still hopeless, even with a little girl on the way. The kicks and flips of my daughter in her mother's womb as I read to her give me the motivation to persevere, along with the promises of the scripture. I still believe them; I'm just waiting to reap them.

So, I yield my life and accept God's authority over me, whole heartedly. I submit my family to Him. I pray that God leads my family in the proper direction. But I do not submit to my calling to preach.

Not now.

I can't bear it.

Robert A. Douglas

The Hard Place

And we know that all things work together for good to them that love God, to them who are the called according to His purpose.
–Romans 8:28

The Countdown

There are only two ways to live your life. One is as though nothing is a miracle. The other is as though everything is a miracle.
-Albert Einstein

"HERE COMES ANOTHER CONTRACTION. PUSH!" comes from Kelly, the nurse.

"1...2...3...4...5...6...7...8...9...10," I help Ashley count. She is doing great. Here comes another, "1...2...3...4...5."

"Robert, there is her head. Look," Dr. Jones guides me. I see black, silky hair entangling blood clots and mucous-like fluids. I can't handle this. The sight and the event is all beautiful, like no other—a miracle. It is the pressure I cannot take. The pressure of becoming a dad, which no one will understand but a dad, sends my mind racing around the track of my life.

School, I have to finish. I have to. Ashley's rapid approach to conquering the university for herself is convincing enough. She gets pregnant, she battles the nausea, she endures the mood swings, the sometimes sleepless nights, the commute from Baltimore to College Park, the extensive amount of walking to and from class on campus, and works an average of thirty hours a week; she manages the many doctor's appointments (especially after we are told our daughter has an irregular heartbeat) and the interviewing process to be employed through Teach For America—in addition to pulling in grades predominately B or higher while taking eighteen credits. Now on her winter break, she is laying on this table pushing out the human she has carried and cared for through it all. She is determined to take the PRAXIS test she is scheduled for the day after she is discharged from the hospital. Her final semester begins in just a few weeks. That is determination.

Whatever the motivation, it is enough to push her to be someone our daughter can look up to. At least she can look up to one of us. For me though, a seven thousand dollar debt is the largest obstacle, but not the only thing that keeps me from finishing school. What will I study? Criminal justice will be a waste of my time. It is not my field, not my calling. Social justices—justice for the hood, justice for hurting people all over the world—are in my field. The broken hearts and damaged souls of our people, poor and rich, are in need of mending and reconciliation. My duty is to help get them to the place of relief. But there is no such study. Psychology does not quite embody the horizon I speak of. Neither do majors like sociology or focuses such as social work. There is no career track for this desire. I must blaze the trail for myself and others.

How?

"6...7...8...9," I continue.

Ministry caters to this desire only partially. Sadly, the modern day church only targets two specific audiences: those who are saved or are trying to be saved. I love the atheists too, and the Muslims, the Jews, the Buddhists, and everyone else traveling along the same dirt paths as I. The growth of what I plan to birth is bigger than the four walls of a church building and the traditionalism that remains trapped within. Besides, ministry does not pay the bills and I must feed my family. So, I need something in addition to that. If a man does not work, he does not eat. I know what it is like to go hungry, but I will not allow my family to experience it. My career must not only sustain my two girls who lay here, one in another, but fulfill my burning passions and be honorable enough and respectable. The Baltimore County Fire Department has not called me with a response to my final interview. I can proudly say I finished the entire process. I have a job now that maintains our livelihood, but I am afraid that it may not much longer with our new addition. People throw at me every occupational opportunity presented these days as if I am not trying myself. I am trying, trying to make a way to experience contentment for what I do best—affecting change.

What is that way?

"10! Good Ash," I finish. She's catching her breath. I am catching mine. The baby slides back up the birthing canal. I've never seen this level of strength in this woman like now. Calmly, I reassure her that she is doing beautifully, to make it appear as if I am as well.

"I feel like I need to push," Ashley tells the doctor.

"O.K."

I see the baby's head again and start the count, "Ready? 1...2." Her head protrudes out further.

What will she look like? Who will she be like? Most importantly, what kind of father will I be?

I look around the delivery room and see all of Ashley's relatives present: her sister, mother, and grandmother. The living members of my ancestry are absent, the deceased in attendance. I text the ones I have telephone numbers for and only receive a response from Marcus saying, "I'm on my way." I'm ok though. I carry Mom on my back everywhere I step foot because I draw my strength from God and my remembrance of her. Grandma, I hoist up on my shoulders because the biblical principles she instilled in me at a young age never left, so she is right below the head, which is Christ. Uncle Antoine and Shontee I have in my arms and Danny, of course, in my heart. They are always with me. I expected someone from the living generations to show up at the hospital or at least call. It is just a false hope and I have no one to blame but myself because they didn't even respond to the baby shower invitations or show up to the event. I hurt myself by breeding the thought that they would view my daughter as a separate entity.

It took everything within me not to deny my daughter her right to meet her family. Yet, they waive their right to meet her. Regardless of how they may feel about me, rightfully so or not, she herself is a member of their family. But they don't care to see that. The only reason I do is because one day she will ask the tough questions in regards to her father's side of the family. Also, as much as I denied it while growing up, I need a source of family. It is a bond that I witness in the lives of others that I long to have. Families are filled with older generations who have gone through the same struggles the younger generations now face. They love the younger enough to impart their wisdom and knowledge in given situations. I am building a family of people who are not my blood, but I am still not experienced enough to possess such wisdom to keep me grounded. My life has been trial and error.

So Moriah's daddy not only lacks college education and a career, but a functioning family as well.

"3...4...5," I continue to count while she pushes.

A change must be made, but where to begin? It's not that I believe a degree is at the pinnacle of success or it somehow validates me as being worthy of opportunities set aside for the "elite."

A piece of paper will not bring peace and does not measure my level of intelligence by any means. It is more of a burning desire to accomplish the goal I originally set out to conquer. Also, operating in a world that is driven on such documentation, it is necessary to an extent for social advancement. But I know that when I depart this earth, it will remain here. So, the ink holds no value.

"6...7," my vocals rush out.

I think I will attend community college. I don't have to have my bill paid in full before I enroll there. Yes, I will do that. This way I can work to improve the marks on my transcript, ease back into the groove of classes, and gradually pay off my bill so by the time I graduate, my debt will be settled and my transition to a four-year university will be smooth.

"8...9," my voice raises.

Fatherhood is nearing. Philosophy will be my major. Eventually, I will go on to...

"10!" I interrupt my thoughts and yell in excitement because her head is out. For some reason, she is blue, her eyes are closed and she is quiet. I grab Ashley's hand.

I have to find my siblings. I miss them dearly. It's been too long since I've seen my little sister's smile or heard my little brother's laughter. Distance has neither distorted those memories nor taken away the fact that they mean the world to me. They are all of my mother that I have left. I have to locate De'Asia and fulfill my promises to Danny also. That little girl needs me. I need her; she is all of Danny I have left. I will honor my word. I will honor my duty as her uncle, as an older brother to my brother and sister and as a cousin to Shontee's children, whom I must find too. Family shouldn't be scattered this way. But can I be the example I need to be for all of these people?

"O.K., stop pushing for a second, Ashley," we hear from Dr. Jones. I see her unwrap the umbilical cord from around our baby's neck. Moriah is still unresponsive. "Now, push."

Moriah Nicole Douglas enters the world on January 12th, 2011 at 1:15p.m. at Mercy Medical Center., still discolored and mute. The doctor places her on Ashley's chest briefly for me to cut the cord. Blood paints my shirt, her grandmother's shoes, the ceiling and the rest of the room as it splatters. Then, they remove her.

"Why isn't she crying?" Ashley cries out.

We all join in tears—tears of joy as we hear the first yelp of my baby love.

Fertile Concrete

It is the seed that produces the harvest—not the farmer or the land.
-Robert Arthur Douglas

SEEDS ARE USUALLY SOWN INTO a land that promises a plentiful harvest. Rarely do they yield in a dry, brittle ground— never in concrete. If concrete could ever render something other than strangling weeds and poisonous ivy, special care would be required. So logically, to reap benefit, a promising area is considered a more worthwhile investment.

A seed rests in the concrete jungle that has only potential— the potential to grow. In the cracks of such a desolate place, no one expects anything beautiful to come from it. Without an adequate environment, it will surely amount to nothing. There are many seeds like this one, resting in the cracks of America's concrete jungles.

So, because it won't prosper, people trample over it, scattering dirt, dust, and dung all around it. The harsh winds from the breath of those who damn it whisk through the debris and make this seed brittle. Everyone sees the dirt, smells the dung, but the seed goes unnoticed. Those who see potential suggest that a seed squandered in such harsh conditions would only grow to be a product of its environment at most—nothing.

Many have given up on this seed or, more importantly, on this jungle. It's surrounded by other seeds battling to make it to the surface prematurely. Its only influence is to strive to do the same.

Then, here comes the blistering cold and heartless rains. They both seep through the dirt. When it rains in these areas, it pours. Already flooded with pain, alone in this muck, beneath the grey clouds where God hides His face, hope withers away. More storms bring more grief, more dirt, more scum for added pressure.

It will never reach the surface, will never break free.

Rarely does the sunshine rise to dry the dirt around these parts. When it does, this once hallow seed can feel the growth and expansion of its insides that no one can see.

Even after experiencing this change, it can't help but notice it is still pressed between the confining walls of the rock hard concrete and the dirt that forces it to remain in between the two, unable to get to the hard place—the surface.

More rain loosens the dirt, feeds it. More sun causes it to grow. People thought kicking dirt would hurt the seed, but it serves as a source for its minerals and nutrients. The dung and feces that were meant to humiliate and degrade both it and its environment is a natural fertilizer to aid in its growth. As horrific as the smell is and uncomfortable as the storms are, they empower the seed to defy all that people said it could never be.

Still, no one can see.

They talk about this lost and fruitless seed as they pass through the jungle. But the strength in what has already developed in the dirt is greater than some that already broke the surface in the grassiest of lands.

Inching its way up each day, it grows closer.

However, it has yet to break that barrier to freedom. It is more deeply rooted than others.

As tangled and starved of oxygen as things can be, it yields what it can from its given circumstance. It may never grow to be greater or more beautiful than others, but one day, it will reach the surface for the world to know that even in such a concrete jungle, it's in the cracks of life that you truly grow.

So grow. Let's break the surface together.

To Be Continued...

Works Used

— The following scriptures: Genesis 4:9, Exodus 20:10, 2 Samuel 22:12, Proverbs 13:22, Proverbs 16:5, Lamentations 3:1-3, Isaiah 54:7-8, Romans 8:28, Romans 8:38-39, James 1:8, and James 4:7 are from the Holy Bible, King James Version.

— The following scriptures: Numbers 30:2, Dueteronomy 23:23, Ecclesiastes 5:4, and Matthew 5:33-37 are from the Holy Bible, New American Standard Version.

— Niebuhr, Reinhold. "The Serenity Prayer." http://www. prayerguide.org.uk/serenity.htm

— Frost, Robert. "Stopping By Woods On A Snowy Evening.: http://www.sparknotes.com/poetry/frost/section10.rhtml

— Pinliard, Arthur. The Way and its Power: A Study of Tao Te Ching and its Place in Chinese Thought. New York.Grove Press Inc. 1958.

— Ritz, David. West, Cornel. Living and Loving Out Loud. Smiley Books. 2009

— All other common and undocumented quotes come from www. great-quotes.com or www.thinkexist.com

Acknowledgements

First and foremost, I give all glory and honor to my personal Lord and Savior, Jesus the Christ. Without you, God, I would have surely lost my life by now and may have taken some. You never gave up on me and you never allowed me to get in too deep. Thank you. I love you, and I owe you my life.

This space is not sufficient to give credit to those who deserve it. If I omit some deserving soul, please count it to my head, not my heart. And know that even if it is not mentioned in this book, I recognize and appreciate you.

I want to thank the team that invested in this project. Andrew McBee, my editor and writing coach. Because of you, I discovered a passion for writing. You helped nurture this gift for years now. Thank you for slaving over this piece of work time-and-time again and supporting this vision. Morgan France-Johnson, my book cover designer. I couldn't have found anyone more talented to invest so fervently into my vision. Your innovative eye will carry you to your destiny. Thank you. Alex Hairston, one of my selfpublishing advisors and sample readers. You didn't grow tired of me picking your brain for information and contacts to make this dream happen. It was all readily available to help ease the process as much as possible. Thank you. Towanda Parker, my other selfpublishing advisor and another sample reader. Thank you for all of your assistance with the business aspect of self-publishing. Only someone who knows the process realizes the tiring efforts that have to go forth in order to make this dream come true. Without your help, it may not have happened this soon. Thank you. Komi Akoumany, my web designer. The website is very much a part of this book. I admire your style, craft, and the wisdom you shared with me in this process and appreciate your support. Thank you brother. Nija Parker, my photographer and a sample reader. You have a passion and you have parents that support you. Dream big and go far. Oh, and thank you for climbing into a river to take pictures of me that we didn't get to use. Thanks for the awesome picture on the back cover as well. Lastly, thanks to all of the sample readers who offered their feedback and advice: Kim Hairston, Meshaunia Vaughn, Shadell Wiggins, Linda Lombardi, Sherri Addison, Delvonda Smith, Eddie and T'Naija Gormley, and the people mentioned above and below who were my sample readers, your words of criticism, wisdom, encouragement, and advice helped this work make it this far. Words cannot express my gratitude to you all.

Mark Miazga. Your job title called for you to teach me English I and English III in high school. You were not hired to shelter me when I had no place to go. It was not in your job description to purchase me a computer and books for my first year of college. But you did it all. You even proofread my college level English papers in your spare time and never spoke of compensation. Thank you. Even though my college career is not yet complete, I promised you I would finish and I plan to fulfill that promise. I thank God for you. You showed me that there are good people in this world. So, I aim to be that someone to a hopeless kid, like you were to me.

The Parkers. I could ramble all day about the aid you provided me over the last four years. Thank you all for your help and support in my time of need. You barely knew me when you first opened your doors to me, but you trusted Ashley Parker enough to help me. Ashley, thank you for standing in the gap for me, for being my best friend, and for supporting me in all that I do. Special thanks to Nasasha Tawanda Parker. No one has ever helped me more than you have. I lived with you for two years and you never asked for a dime, even when I was working at the jobs you helped me get. You knew I was depressed and that I gave up on my life so you didn't push me too much, but also didn't allow me to lay around and sulk. We have been there for one another in many ways and as I've told you—any day, anywhere, any time. Thanks.

If all of my struggles were to get me on the path to meet Hazel Brashears, it was well worth it. Granny Hazel, you love me like a grandson and you are so spiritually enlightened. You saw God working in me and knew after meeting me just a few times that I was destined for greatness. I love you and I thank you for all you have been to me in my life. More importantly, thank you for believing in me and investing in my life.

To these people, I love you and thank you for everything: Bernard Leneau and my entire wrestling team, Sgt. Nelson Moody Jr., Nathaniel Larimore, Rodney Joyner, Marcus Smothers, my co-workers and supervisors at the Arc of Howard County, and everyone from the streets that accepted me even when I chose to reform and walk the path God set out for me.

Last but not least, I thank you—the reader. My life has been put on display for you. It was so tough writing this book. But I was convinced that it would help someone, someday. I hope it has helped you to release the emotions of the past in order to set you free. We all have struggles. In this day and age, we live to uphold reputations

Sfrt*Fertile Concrete: A Memoir*

and images that do not allow us to be as transparent as we would like. I would love to hear from you personally. Feel free to email me at me@robertadouglas.org. Thanks again to you all and thanks be to God.

140

Made in the USA
Middletown, DE
04 May 2021